The Golden Age of SPORTS CARS

OTHER BOOKS BY LOUIS STEINWEDEL

The Duesenberg: *The Story of America's Premier Car*
Co-author J. Herbert Newport

The Mercedes-Benz Story

The Golden Age of SPORTS CARS

Louis William Steinwedel

CHILTON BOOK COMPANY
Philadelphia New York London

Published in Philadelphia by Chilton Book Company
and simultaneously in Ontario, Canada,
by Thomas Nelson & Sons, Ltd.

ISBN: 0–8019–5691–9
Library of Congress Catalog Card No. 74–187839
Designed by Cypher Associates
Manufactured in the United States of America

This book is dedicated to
my parents,
LOUIS and KATHARINE

Acknowledgments

Many have been generous with their time, energy, and good will in helping to create this book. To them the author expresses his sincere appreciation.

Alfa Romeo, Milano

Mr. Al Bloemker, Indianapolis Motor Speedway Corp.

Mr. Jean R. Broncard, Automobiles Peugeot, Paris

Mr. John W. Burgess, Sr., Director, Briggs Cunningham Automotive Museum

Count Marcus Clary, Director of Special Programs, Mercedes-Benz of North America, Inc., and the Daimler-Benz Archives, Stuttgart

Mr. M. L. Bud Cohn, Los Angeles, California

Mr. Eric Dahlquist, Editor, *Motor Trend* magazine, Petersen Publishing Co.

Mr. John Durand, Photographer, Baltimore, Maryland

Harrah's Automobile Collection, Mr. E. R. Tarnowsky, Director of Public Relations, Reno, Nevada

Mr. Buddy Hoelzeman, Manager, The Museum of Automobiles, Morrilton, Arkansas
Mr. Ed Jurist, The Vintage Car Store, Nyack, New York
Mr. Charles B. McCabe, General Motors Overseas Operations
Montagu Motor Museum, Mr. E. A. Bellamy
Mr. J. Kuba, Director, National Technical Museum, Prague
Mr. D. E. A. Miller-Williams, Rolls-Royce Motors, Ltd, London
Mr. J. Herbert Newport
Mr. Enzo Stuarti

The author acknowledges the special generosity of Mr. William H. Thomas, Jr., and Mr. Josef Riedlbauer of Aisquith Auto Service, Baltimore, Maryland

Louis William Steinwedel

Baltimore, Maryland 1971

Contents

Chapter 1

RUMBLINGS, RAMBLINGS, AND RACES

Sports cars are an enigma not unlike sailing yachts, race horses, antique guns, mountain climbing, and restoring eighteenth century farm houses. There are faster and more comfortable ways of crossing open water than by sail, more solid investments than thoroughbreds, better ways to hunt or target shoot than with a flintlock, less vigorous means of viewing Alpine scenery than by climbing the Matterhorn (helicopter, for one), and less frustrating ways of getting a roof over bed and board than the "Mister Blandings" syndrome. And there are often better ways of getting between Point A and Point B than by driving a sports car: by 747, for instance, if Point A and Point B are relatively distant, and by foot if the two points happen to be Grand Central Station and Times Square at 5:00 P.M. on a Friday. And today, if the points happen to be the intersection of Hollywood and Vine and the Palm Springs Racquet Club, there is unlikely to be much time differential in getting there between the guy who shifts for himself in a 330 GT Ferrari and the fellow who prefers to lounge in the back seat with cognac and companion while the hired help pilots something on the order of a 300 SEL 6.3 litre Mercedes-Benz or a Maserati Quattroporto.

So then, why sports cars? Answering that question, and simply trying to define the sports car, has occupied car fans ever since they discovered that driving such a car can be a much more rewarding experience than simply covering the ground between Points A and B by the most coldly efficient means. With the right car under you, the steel and springs and polished lacquer become more than just transportation—they become an extension of the driver which responds not only to his hand but also to his psyche. Sports cars, as a rule, tend to do this sort of responding—both physically and psychologically—rather better than the average commuter's sedan. If there must be a *raison d'être* for the sports car it is simply that it is a car totally conceived for the *pleasure* of spirited driving. Contrary to the popular misconception, the emphasis in a true sports car is not nearly so much on raw power as it is on handling, suspension, and roadability. It is this difference which makes even a little Austin-Healey Sprite or Fiat 850 a sports car in spite of the fact that an ordinary Buick or Cadillac can leave it in the dust for acceleration and top speed, at least on a straight road.

Today's great sports cars—Ferrari, Maserati, Mercedes-Benz, Jaguar, Aston-Martin, Alfa Romeo—represent one of man's most consistently refined contrivances, perfected and polished with reverent devotion over many years. Technology and production techniques have also made quite good low priced sports cars widely available, which are in some ways equal or even superior to many of the expensive sports cars of the past.

So then, why *classic* sports cars? It should be obvious that a sports car must properly be a very personal thing, a reflection of one's individuality. So, it follows that many of the great sports cars were created by staunch individualists. Unfortunately, truly individualistic artist-engineers find today's world of colossal corporations, computers, and cut-throat competition a rough and inhospitable climate. It is seldom a safe world for loners with an idea and a special point of view. So,

A pioneer Peugeot, 1891.

AUTOMOBILES PEUGEOT

conversely, it is no surprise that one and perhaps the last of a long school of such loners—Enzo Ferrari—has produced some of the most successful, electrifying, and best loved sports cars of the past quarter century.

In the infancy and adolescence of the sports car many more such men also worked without the necessity of a total regard for what other builders were doing—and sometimes with a total disregard. Ettore Bugatti, that arch individualist of them all, did not consider it at all odd, for example, to build a car (the Type 46) in which the rear axle and crankshaft had to be dismounted in order to inspect the valves. Likewise, he did not consider it odd or unusual that his cars should score over a thousand successes in the racing seasons of 1925–26 alone. Bugatti and a select few of his fellow creative engineers of the day followed their own dictates.

Such men as Bugatti, Wilhelm Maybach, Marc Birkigt and a few others were building true sports cars before World War I, although the term itself did not come into general use until the 1920s. However, it was this period between the wars which was really to become The Golden Age of Sports Cars.

Several circumstances conspired to set the stage for greatness. The basic research to bring the automobile to a fairly reliable state of development had been done prior to World War I. But the emphasis of wartime development, particularly in metallurgy and increased engine efficiency for the more stringent requirements of aircraft engines (and the perfection of supercharging), brought the state-of-the-art to new heights of sophistication in the 1920s. Coupled with the new technical knowledge was an abundance of creative engineering talent to use it and of skilled, low-cost artisans to put the cars into production. Further, sufficient war profits and prosperity

In July 1894 the French newspaper *Le Petit Journal* organized a trial run "pour les voitures sans chevaux." The event attracted 102 entries, among them this vis-à-vis Peugeot, and is sometimes thought of as the world's first automobile race.

AUTOMOBILES PEUGEOT

existed on both sides of the Atlantic to enable buyers to pay for them (for awhile, anyway), and sufficient taste and selectivity lingered from the patrician Edwardian age to assure genuine appreciation of them. The cars produced by this unique confluence of circumstances—and particularly the sports cars—were epic. It is these cars themselves, which sometimes diffuse the line between craft and art, that answer the question "Why classic sports cars?"

To fully understand and appreciate the best of The Golden Age of Sports Cars it is necessary to go back into the origins of the sports car and lay some groundwork. In the beginning, any car that could run with some degree of reliability was a "sporting" car and the owners of such wondrous machines couldn't resist the opportunity to challenge each other in daring displays of speed and skill in which the fearsome velocity of ten or twelve miles an hour might be breached. As a Frenchman observed near the turn of the century, "To see a car pass at racing speed—some of these little machines can spurt at twenty miles an hour—takes one's breath away. The apparition is uncanny."

Certainly, you could go faster more comfortably in a very ordinary railway coach but riding high above the road on a rickety buggy-like contraption that panted from one or two small cylinders offered a far more sporting sensation of speed. It could be a risky affair, but after all wasn't it the uncertainty that made it sporting in the first place? The early races served two worthwhile purposes. They did a lot to introduce the infant automobile, and they were, on occasion, immense fountains of public entertainment. Automobile racing is a bit older than most people guess and it grew to mass popularity at an early age. Even before the nineteenth century was out cars could top 65 mph and thousands of people turned out to see them run.

A French auto trial from Neuilly-sur-Seine in the Paris suburbs to Rouen in 1894 is memorable because it was the first formal gathering of automobiles. The event was organized by a newspaper called *Le Petit Journal* which put up a first prize of five thousand francs to be awarded to "la voiture sans chevaux" (horseless carriage) which best satisfied the conditions of being "without danger," easily operated by the driver, and run with reasonable economy. There were 102 entries, but only twenty-one cars actually started out to demonstrate their reliability over the seventy-five miles of white pebbled roads between Neuilly and Rouen. To people who regard the Model T as a venerable antiquity it seems curious that while the blue coated U.S. Cavalry was still fighting Indians the French were conducting a serious automobile reliability run. It is an interesting clash of images.

Promptly at 8:30 on a sunny summer morning, July 22nd 1894, the twenty-one cars started out. Actually, the event was conceived by Pierre Griffard, the director of *Le Petit Journal*, as a Concours and trial, and hopefully as a demonstration of the seriousness and utility of the new automobiles. However, the competitive aspects of the run have been emphasized over the years and it is occasionally thought of as "the world's first automobile race," which is not really an accurate description. But it didn't take the French much more than a few months to get around to all-out racing.

The early steam cars largely dominated the Paris-Rouen, from the standpoints of both performance and hilarity. Although a De Dion "steam tractor" was the fastest vehicle in the race at 11.5 mph average speed, any glory the steam fanciers may have derived from this record was overcome by the comedy of the steam cars. Despite the danger, the sight of poorly steered steamers scattering throngs of the curious (who dodged them like torreros), demolishing obstacles in their paths, and showering spectators with hails of pebbles kicked up from the road lent a comic flavor to the day.

A French auto trial from Paris to Rouen in 1894 is memorable because it was the first formal gathering of automobiles. The event was organized by *Le Petit Journal* which put up a prize of five thousand francs to be awarded to *la voiture sans chevaux* which best satisfied the conditions.

Le Petit Journal

TOUS LES JOURS
Le Petit Journal
5 Centimes

SUPPLÉMENT ILLUSTRÉ
Huit pages : CINQ centimes

TOUS LES DIMANCHES
Le Supplément illustré
5 Centimes

nquième année — LUNDI 6 AOUT 1894 — Numéro 194

Concours du « Petit Journal »
LES VOITURES SANS CHEVAUX

A few years earlier Count Albert De Dion had taken an interest in a young engineer named George Bouton who was unalterably convinced that the future of the road machine lay in steam. He was not alone. In America, the Stanley brothers thought so, too, and by 1906 had an aerodynamically shaped racing car that shot over the sands of Daytona Beach at a dazzling speed of well over a hundred miles an hour. Very impressive—until it took off, flew for a short distance, and crashed back to earth. Steam did have its advantages and at least one steamer, the prestigious Doble, was built in America into the 1930s.

The result of the De Dion-Bouton alliance was the "steam tractor" which reached Rouen five hours and forty minutes

In the beginning they were all sports cars. This one is an 1893 Benz "Velo," the 27th car built. The Benz Velo was the world's first series-produced car and this one is the oldest running specimen.

COLLECTION OF M. L. BUD COHN

after it left Neuilly, the fastest time of the twenty-one participants. The De Dion-Bouton could hardly have been called a car; it was more like a small trackless locomotive pulling an open Victoria carriage for the passengers. The judges had some late misgivings about the crude but successful half car-half train. They questioned the propriety of a steamer in an "automobile" trial, and they questioned whether it was really "easily managed by the driver" as required by Article 6 of the rules. After some animated, percussive French had rent the air they decided to give it second prize, even though it had the best time, and they awarded first prize to one of Armand Peugeot's six cars which had recorded second best time. Perfectly understandable Gallic logic. The Daimler-engined Peugeots were the most sophisticated cars in the run. The winning car had a Vee-design, two-cylinder engine of 75 x 140 mm bore and stroke which could push it well over 12 mph and it put out about 3½ hp. Everyone was a bit confused, however, when the judges decided that a Panhard-Levassor also with a Daimler engine had really performed equally as well as the Peugeot and deserved some recognition. So they gave it equal glory with the Peugeot and both of them split the five thousand francs prize money. This was the very same year that French justice sent Captain Dreyfus to Devil's Island, but apparently *justice, egalité, fraternité* was still available for motorcars.

It was no accident that the world's first celebrated automobile trial took place amidst the green panorama of *la belle France*. The automobile had technically been born in Germany nine years before with the first practical internal combustion engines of Gottlieb Daimler and Karl Benz, but it was in France that the automobile took its first few steps. The reason was basically freedom, both physical and legal. Like the Caesars, Napoleon realized the military and civil importance of good roads. Railroads later reduced the need somewhat but by the time the automobile came along the Emperor's highways were still there. They were not much by modern standards, but they were Europe's best and no one seemed to object to running automobiles on them. To the early drivers they were free and unobstructed paths to glory, unlike England's highways and the infamous "Red Flag Law" which required that a man walk ahead of an automobile, waving a red flag to warn of its approach at the legal limit of four miles an hour—two miles an hour in town. It would still be two years after the Paris-Rouen until the conservative English repealed the rule, and even then the prejudice against motorists lingered on. It was a sad start for a country which was to become one of the most sports car minded in the world, but perhaps people remembered that the world's first fatal automobile accident happened in Britain in 1834 when Scott Russell's "steam carriage" blew up and killed five people in Glasgow. A driver's license could cost an Englishman up to about $50.00 and it was good only in the one county which issued it. The English were very particular about their driving licenses and there were many formalities. However, the ability to see where you were going was not one of them, as a motoring journal pointed out when it obtained a perfectly legal license for a blind man. Similar barriers existed in America, where early motorcars were resented as rich men's toys. Even years later when cars were fairly commonplace Woodrow Wilson would claim that "Nothing has spread socialistic feeling in this country more than the use of the automobile, which is a picture of the arrogance of wealth with all its independence and carelessness." But the chief drawback to early American cars was the deplorable state of roads beyond the cobblestone city streets, sorry deep cuts of alternate mud or dust fit only for high wheeled farm wagons.

Nevertheless, America was not to be outdone by France. The new owner of the *Chicago Times-Herald*, H. H. Kohlsaat, decided that if the French could organize an automobile trial he could put on an automobile *race*, and he promised $5000 in prize money, with $2000 as first prize. Then Kohlsaat set about organizing and publicizing his great race, the biggest thing to hit Chicago since the great fire. He ran a separate contest with a prize of $500 to select a proper name for the new machines that were to race to fame and fortune. The French *automobile* and German *Motorwagen* were much too foreign for middle America. Response to Kohlsaat's promotion was encouraging. About eighty cars were entered for the first American automobile race which was to be run on the Fourth of July 1895. Everything looked fine until a few weeks before the festivities when Mr. Kohlsaat learned that most of the entrants had great enthusiasm for racing, but that few of them had automobiles. The great race was reluctantly postponed until Thanksgiving Day and even by then only half a dozen "motorcycles"—the name chosen by the contest judges—were ready to race.

The brothers Duryea, Frank and Charles, were there from Massachusetts with their new twin-cylinder car which was claimed to be capable of 16 mph. The Duryeas brought with them the prestige of the first successful American gasoline automobile, although they had leaned heavily on German innovation for their original one-cylinder "buggyaut" of 1892–93. This new car for the Chicago race was an improved version but remained faithful to the Benz concepts. According to the *Scientific American* for December 1895, "The paternity of the motor vehicle of Charles Duryea is admittedly that of Karl Benz." Other builders were similarly influenced by the moustached mechanic from Mannheim: the early King car was Benz in theory and the Winton was openly called "a Benz copy." Benz himself was fairly well represented in the Chicago race. On race day there were three original cars with Benz engines at the starting line. One was entered by R. H. Macy of New York, another by H. Mueller & Co. of Decatur, Illinois, and the third by De La Verne Refrigerating Co. of New York. The final two cars in the small field were electrics: the "Sturgess Electric Motorcycle" and the Morriss & Salom entry from Philadelphia.

Thanksgiving Day of 1895 dawned bright and clear in Chicago and thousands of spectators were out on the streets to catch their first glimpse of a real "motorcycle." Even the several inches of snow which had fallen the night before did not chill the enthusiasm. The start required a little over an hour and one by one the half dozen cars struggled valiantly off over the snow. If the steamers in the Paris-Rouen the previous summer had been the comic sensation of the season, then the Chicago race was the opposite number in pathos, for the primitive, cold, little machines made a pathetic picture picking their way over the snowy route. There was little excitement and the cold crowds were more curious than captivated. A smattering of applause broke out when Frank Duryea caught and passed the leading Macy Benz on Forest Avenue. A little later a horse cab refused to yield the right of way to the Macy Benz and it came away from the disagreement with a damaged front wheel and a badly bent steering gear. O'Connor, the driver, pushed it on anyway—using the streetcar tracks to keep the wheels straight part of the way—and despite a scanty knowledge of the route he brought it home third.

Frank Duryea rolled along satisfyingly well with his brother Charles following behind in a one-horse open sleigh just in case. As the day grew dim the race narrowed to Duryea and the Mueller Benz. Then Duryea made a wrong turn at Lawrence Avenue which cost him about two miles. But it did not cost him the lead because the Mueller Benz had broken its drive belt and stopped for repairs. At 7:18 that evening the twelve hundred pound dual cylinder Duryea won the first American automobile race, although only a hardy few frostbitten souls were on hand to witness the victory.

The Chicago race whetted the American appetite for the new automobile. The Duryeas went on to win the Cosmopolitan Race from New York City to Irvington with the same twin-cylinder car in 1896. An interesting feature of the Duryea car was that its twin cylinders were independent of each other: if half of the engine failed the car would still run on the other half. It also had a rudimentary transmission which gave four speeds. The Duryeas added one more first to their list of accomplishments when they started to produce the same car in series, but only thirteen were built. The runner-up

Mueller Benz went touring through Illinois in the Spring of 1896 and was the first horseless carriage ever seen by thousands of Americans. It rated a torchlight parade in Indianapolis and at election time it carried William Jennings Bryan on part of his campaign.

It is hard to think of the spindly, buggy-like Daimlers, Peugeots, Duryeas, Benzes, Panhards and the rest of their nineteenth century contemporaries as sports cars. Yet to the young men of those days they were as exciting and dashing as the cars of Ettore Bugatti and Walter Owen Bentley were to their sons in the 1920s, and as modern and sleek as Enzo Ferrari's creations are to their grandsons in the 1970s. Almost from the beginning the automobile was a sporting proposition. A few publicity conscious businessmen used gas-powered vehicles for delivery (the Bon Marche department store in Paris used a Benz delivery truck in 1896), or as taxis. And Gottlieb Daimler had his engines in an internal combustion streetcar by 1889, in an airship the year before, a narrow-gauge locomotive in 1890, and a fire engine in 1892. But the average fellow was often unimpressed with such workaday utility. A horse and buggy would get him to town on Saturday night, the railroad would haul his freight, and a team of Clydesdales would bring him his beer. But an automobile, ah!, that was no workhorse. It was something to ride in for fun, to show off, to race down a dusty lane or a cobblestone avenue while everyone watched. To drive was not work but a thrilling new sport, and those who could afford it thought that the automobile should be developed around that idea. American mass production techniques would put an early death to such views in the United States and by World War I the domestic sports car admirer had begun to settle for the Sunday afternoon drive. Some Europeans, however, had other ideas.

Chapter 2

THE FEVER TAKES HOLD

Despite the hassle at the finish line, the race from Paris to Rouen in 1894 was such a popular success and conversation piece in the cafes and bistros that *Le Petit Journal* decided to sponsor another race the following year. This one would be a bit more ambitious: south from Paris through the gentle chateau country of the Loire valley and the vineyards of Guyenne and back to Paris, an optimistically long 732 miles. The field was much smaller this time with only twenty-two cars, but considerably more sophisticated after a year of testing, re-designing, and re-building. On June 11th 1895 a waving crowd saw the racers off and thousands of curious spectators waited along the way as the drivers "teuf-teufed" past at sedate speeds which seemed to match their prim Victorian sartorial propriety. Auto racing was still a formal affair which called for collar, cravat, and a bowler hat; the twenty-two drivers all looked like Toulouse-Lautrec.

The pace was promptly set by Emile Levassor in his sporty two-seater Panhard with a 1.2 litre four-horsepower engine. The little car was capable of nearly 20 mph top speed, and when Levassor rolled back into the Paris suburbs 48 hours and

48 minutes later his average speed for the run was an amazing 15 mph, which meant that the car had been running almost flat out all the way. Although the little twin-cylinder engine had been running virtually non-stop for over two days the trip was completely trouble-free.

Poor Levassor certainly earned the first prize—which he never got. When he reached the control point where his relief driver was supposed to take over he found that the fellow was still asleep somewhere. So Emile gassed up the car, climbed back up, and made the complete run himself, spending nearly fifty-three hours in the car. By any standard Levassor was the best man with the best car on that day in 1895, but the eligibility rules called for four-seater cars only. So it was the next car, a Peugeot that arrived six hours later, which officially got credit for winning the Paris-Bordeaux race. Actually, Levassor had known the rules ahead of time, so he hadn't really (as the phrase goes) snatched defeat from the jaws of victory the way Count De Dion had done the year before. Levassor had set out to prove his car and himself and he was satisfied with the result, in spite of what the record book read.

The Paris-Bordeaux of 1895 was a milestone in automotive history for two reasons. First, it showed conclusively that the infant automobile could be reliable and practical—more than an amusing toy. And at the same time the race signaled the rise of the new internal combustion engine over the old steamer. Six steamers were in the race, the favorite being Amedee Bollee's "steam bus." Bollee came to the starting line with the confidence of over two decades of building successful steam cars. His confidence was well founded; his very first car back in 1873 could have outrun the fastest gas-powered car in the field, and his newest entry was a six passenger machine which was good for up to 40 mph. But the odds against Bollee grew with the miles to Bordeaux. Steamers were fine and fast for short distances but, like today's attempts to produce a practical pollution-free steam car, they offered challenges. Bollee's "bus" drank water constantly and

Marcel Renault and his "lightweight class" 16 hp Renault, winner of the 1902 Paris-to-Vienna race. Renault's victory with a small ancestor of the sports car against much larger cars demonstrated that the big engines and brute power of contemporary racing cars did not necessarily make them the fastest cars.

COURTESY RENAULT, INC.

had to make frequent stops. Overheating was another problem, and at one point in the race Bollee wrapped a wet cloth around his boiler to cool things off. Then, when he wasn't looking, the cloth was sucked into the moving machinery. The final result was a ninety-hour time for the run, nearly twice that for Levassor's flawless little internal combustion car.

The curiosity bred by these early races quickly turned to fascination and then into full and fierce Gallic passion. If Germany had been the father of the automobile, France had become its nurturing mother and did everything she could to foster speed spectacles with cars that seemed to develop in size and speed almost daily. French motor passion and prestige soon solidified into the powerful *Automobile Club de France.* The ACF worked hard to promote the automobile in general and racing in particular. It enthusiastically welcomed all comers to race on the good roads of France, but took a paternalistic view in seeing that a French car should have the best chance to finish first.

It was not long before even the open, poplar-lined roads of France became too confining for the new racing machines. Soon the young racing cult erased even national boundaries. In 1898 the racers took off on the first of the colorful capital-

Marcel Renault at speed in the infamous Paris-to-Madrid race of 1903, approaching the curve at Couhe-Verac where the car crashed, Renault killed and his riding mechanic seriously injured. The Paris-Madrid signaled the last of the colorful country-to-country races and ended an era.

COURTESY RENAULT, INC.

to-capital races, the Paris-Amsterdam, and later the more rugged Paris-Berlin. Then in 1902 came one of the most arduous races ever run in any age, the Paris-Vienna.

The course between the gayest cities in ante-bellum Europe ran through the Alps by way of the Arlberg Pass where the roads deteriorated into primitive trails that curled along the lips of spectacular mountains. One wrong turn would see you over the unfenced edge and into a scenic, snowy oblivion. The Paris-Vienna would have been a severe test for a good sports car lifted fifty years out of the future, but the imperious, moustachioed drivers of 1902 were equipped with cars of dubious balance, reluctant two wheel brakes, harsh steering, and suspension carried over from the carriage age. Their tires were pitifully poor things which sometimes offered less mileage than a tank of gas. Even in later races a dozen tire changes in four hundred miles was not unheard of. And "tire change" is just what was meant, for the demountable rim was still four years in the future when the Paris-Vienna was run. When a tire went somewhere along the way the driver and his riding mechanic jumped down to wrench the shredded rubber from the rim and then fit a new tire over the wheel. At best it was a tough and dirty five- or ten-minute job, and the demountable rim—not to mention the knock-off wheel—must have seemed like a gift from heaven when it came along.

The technology for building better suspension, handling, brakes, and tires was advancing, but not nearly so rapidly as the designers' ability to construct bigger and bigger engines to put out more and more horsepower for faster and faster

Renault was one of the early believers in the small, agile "voiturette" or small car which was closer to the concepts of the true sports car than the brutish, large-displacement racing cars of the very early 1900s. Here, a group of four small Renaults lines up for the Paris-to-Bordeaux race of 1902. These cars finished 1-2-3-4 in their "voiturette" or light car class.

COURTESY RENAULT, INC.

A large 90 hp Renault takes a curve in the Dieppe race of 1906.
COURTESY RENAULT, INC.

speeds. The really deadly thing about high performance cars of Paris-Vienna vintage was that their big engines were so much faster than their chassis. It was an ominous trend, and a temptation which some builders have never quite gotten over to this day. With mile-a-minute cars at hand that displaced twelve litres or more, even the motor-loving French began to get a little nervous. For awhile in 1902 the Minister of the Interior banned racing on the public roads. It was a hard blow to sportsmen, but then—as it has a habit of doing—the French government changed hands and all was well for the Paris-Vienna.

Cooler heads who had begun to talk of the "menace of the motorcar" were quickly forgotten in the excitement of the gala start from Paris. In fact, the newfound motor speed captured the popular fancy much like moon flights would nearly three quarters of a century later. A trainload of spectators out from Paris cheered wildly as Henri Fournier on a big wooden-framed Mors blasted by at over 70 mph to leave the train in his dust. Maxi-skirted ladies and black-broadcloth-suited gen-

A Peugeot on the Paris-Bordeaux road in 1895. That year *Le Petit Journal* sponsored a second event, this time over 732 miles of good French roads between Paris and Bordeaux. A Peugeot was the official winner in 54 hours and 32 minutes, and the car above finished about four hours later.

AUTOMOBILES PEUGEOT

tlemen waved and shouted "Formidable!" and "Bonne chance!" It was all very gay, fin-de-siècle, and decorously decadent.

Despite the trail of shattered machinery, egos, and a few bones between Paris and Vienna the Edwardian gaiety managed to prevail in the absence of any real disasters. And the race was not without its lighter moments. One of them happened when a French driver named Genty was heading down an Alpine pass in a big Clement racer, well geared down for the descent. From behind him, piercing even the wind and engine noise, came a cry of terror. He looked back to see a wildly gesturing fellow on a motorcycle whose brakes had failed. The gap between them was closing fast. As the cyclist pulled alongside the Clement, Genty reached out and grabbed his coat collar and dragged him aboard as the cycle shot out from under him and disappeared over the edge of a cliff. The humor probably escaped the poor cyclist but the whole scene must have been pure Keystone Cops.

The lesson of the Paris-Vienna was clearly that big engines and brute power alone do not make "fast" cars, particularly over terrain like the Austrian Alps. Like most of the early races, the Paris-Vienna was run in classes according to maximum weight rather than displacement or horsepower and a wide variety of "light" and "heavy" cars competed with each other. Popular interest generally ran with the high-powered big cars, with the small cars forming part of the background, like the smaller sports cars at Le Mans today. But—the race was an upset, won by one of these small cars in a clean-cut, decisive victory. Marcel Renault's "light weight class" 16 hp Renault did the route in 15 hours and 45 minutes at the incredible average of 38.9 mph. Renault's time was nearly an hour better than that of the next car to finish, Henry Farman's favored giant 70 hp Panhard.

It was handwriting on the wall—that a smaller, well developed car could hold an advantage over a bigger and more powerful car—but a lot of people chose not to read the message. Instead of revising their cars the racers revised the route to better suit the cars, which appeared the next year with

Peugeot driver M. Petit glances back at his competition in the Bordeaux-to-Agen race in May 1898. Petit won, covering the 138 kilometers in 3 hours and 1 minute.

AUTOMOBILES PEUGEOT

Peugeot in the Marseille-to-Nice race in March 1898.

AUTOMOBILES PEUGEOT

even more displacement and raw power and even lighter chassis. For 1903 the route combined the fine, flat roads of France with the horrible roads of Spain, and the promise was for the greatest automobile race in history, a grand super spectacle of over two hundred cars racing from Paris to Madrid.

Teams prepared for the Paris-Madrid as they never had before; the French paper *La Presse* reported that "French automobile constructors spent $10,000,000 over their preparation." Rivalries, both commercial and now national, were rising and the pressure to win rose with them. But under the glamour and gaiety ran an ominous current. The German

The "voiturettes" or small, light cars pioneered by the French were the ancestors of true sports cars, offering speed plus maneuverability. Here, a Lion-Peugeot is on the way to victory in the Coupe des Voiturettes of the Circuit de Lombardie.

AUTOMOBILES PEUGEOT

motoring newspaper *Allgemeine Automobil Zeitung* sensed this and wrote a strangely prophetic editorial, which was generally ignored. The writer referred to Count Zborowski's recent death on a Sixty Mercedes at Nice, plus several other fatal accidents in high powered cars, and continued: "When I think that perhaps 250 cars will start in the Paris-Madrid race, and that at least fifty of these will be provided with such terribly powerful motors, and finally that, of all the drivers probably only twenty are capable of mastering these speed monsters, I feel inclined to pray to Heaven that the race may not be the occasion of some frightful accident. I am no prophet of evil, but if accident on accident should take place in the Paris-Madrid race, what a clamor there would be in

Motoring dress styles changed from the collar, tie and bowler hat of 1894 to this 1905 image of George Heath and his riding mechanic swathed in dusters and goggled and masked, ready to race for the Vanderbilt Cup.

AMERICAN AUTOMOBILE MANUFACTURER'S ASSOCIATION

that section of the press which persistently opposes automobiles."

Zborowski's death earlier in the Spring of 1903 *had* caused quite an anti-automobile commotion. In fact, Monsieur Combes, the French Minister of the Interior, had again banned racing on French roads (right in the middle of Nice Speed Week), but relented in time to let the Paris-Madrid go on. So, at 3:45 on the dark and misty morning of May 24th, 216 drivers with their machines and 300,000 spectators assembled along the Bordeaux road at Versailles. It was as varied a lot of road machinery as had ever been gathered in one place before, and there would never be anything quite like it again. Quaint little 3-hp gas-powered tricycles parked next to fierce 100-hp Gobron-Brillie racers which could put out nearly one mile per hour for each horsepower. That morning's first light fell on an incredible scene which would never be duplicated in the history of motor racing. Back from the big black and white *Départ* banner stretched a long line of cars stripped for speed. They represented the cream of the growing motor industry. On the other side of the banner were dual lines of human heads, packed four and five deep as far as the eye could see, which eventually converged into a solid mass and blotted out the road. The French army, which had been dispatched to control the crowd, was hopelessly overwhelmed and melted into the mob like raindrops in a rushing stream.

The first leg of the race stretched 342 miles from Versailles to Bordeaux, over practically the same route as the 1895 Paris-Bordeaux and supposedly the finest road in France. The second leg was not such smooth sailing: over the Pyrennes and on to Madrid by way of rutted trails hardly changed since Caesar's day. Along the Bordeaux road waited throngs of the curious estimated at up to three million, and few of them had any concept of an automobile moving at 80 or 90 mph.

Vintage motor sport on Long Island; the Vanderbilt Cup race of 1905. The races for Willie K. Vanderbilt's big silver cup brought out as many as 300,000 spectators.

AMERICAN AUTOMOBILE MANUFACTURER'S ASSOCIATION

With little crowd control along the way, it was not long before the mixture of high speed, Latin passion, and near mob psychology began to take its toll. Only a few kilometers from the start the first spectator was hit by a car and thrown back into the crowd. It was only the beginning. Further down the road a soldier rushed out to save a child from an onrushing car and both were hit. In another incident a driver named Tourand swerved to avoid pedestrians and turned his car over,

The Packard "Gray Wolf," designed by Packard's German engineer Charles Schmidt, could have been the prototype of an advanced American sports car, but the small and highly efficient concept was never developed to its potential. The Gray Wolf ran in the 1904 Vanderbilt Cup race with a small 4.5-litre engine a third the size of some rivals, yet it finished fourth. Schmidt's effective design mounted the engine and clutch forward as a single unit with the transmission on the rear axle.

AMERICAN AUTOMOBILE MANUFACTURER'S ASSOCIATION

killing the riding mechanic and several onlookers. Again and again the same horror was repeated. A fast car would appear in the distance and a mass of people waiting somewhere along the route would push forward for a better view and flow over the road like a giant, pulsing amoeba. When a driver saw an immobile mass of frozen faces loom up in front of him and he was closing fast at seventy or eighty he had two quick choices: pull his wheels off the road and probably kill himself or hang onto the steering wheel and pray that they would get out of his way in time. Before the day was over both choices were made many times, with equally disastrous results.

1905 Reo two-seater sports roadster appears as a scaled down version of the all-out racing machines of the day. Car was Grand National Champion at the International Car Show in New York, 1966.

COLLECTION OF M. L. BUD COHN

The great Belgian driver Camille Jenatzy at speed in the 1903 Paris-Madrid in his 90 hp Mercedes at the Petignac Curve. Note the dust clouds, one of the great hazards of classic racing. Shortly afterward, the car was forced to stop by a mangled horsefly in the carburetor.

DAIMLER-BENZ A.G.

The cars in the Paris-Madrid were little less than suicidal by modern sports and racing car standards. Designers had forsaken everything else for speed, speed, and more speed. Cars in the smallest *voiturette* class were limited to from 550 to 880 pounds, in the "light car" class from 880 to 1430 pounds. The "large cars" were unlimited as to both displacement and weight but most designers made every effort to keep them as light as possible, even punching Swiss cheese holes in everything from frames to light brackets and using lightweight caned seats. Some went even further. *The Autocar* had a reporter on the scene who observed: "The weather was warm, but still traveling for hours at speed is not a heating exercise, even on a warm day. Maurice Farman, for instance, started on a big racing Panhard clad in an ordinary light cycling suit, with no overcoat, and in the light *voiturette* class the craving to keep down the weight had evidently spread to the driver and his clothes. To be sure, some of those light *voiturettes* looked as if they only wanted the added weight of a driving coat to bend in two, and how they can stand the vibrations of their powerful motors, to say nothing of the road shocks, is a mystery."

Into these small, frail chassis the engineers of 1903 laid the biggest possible engines. Some of the cars in the race had hulking ten- or twelve-litre engines with more displacement in one of their four cylinders than some modern cars have in their entire engines. With such a combination of overpowered and underengineered cars it was no wonder that some of the drivers who successfully dodged the spectators fell victims to their own cars. A particularly bloody scene was the thirty-seven kilometers between Montguyon and Libourne near the end of the first leg. Here the road curved and twisted and demanded the utmost maneuverability from the hard steering, ill-balanced cars rocketing over it. This stretch of road claimed a heavy toll of cars and drivers who simply lost control at speed or crashed into each other trying to pass. It was here that Lorraine Barrow tried to avoid an obstacle and ran off the road and into a tree at 80 mph. Barrow was thrown sixty feet and died later in a hospital at Libourne and his mechanic was killed instantly. The De Dietrich in which they were riding was as completely destroyed as it is possible for a car to be. Parts of the front suspension and steering were deeply embedded in the tree and the engine was torn out of the frame with its pistons ripped out and shattered. Nearby, Marcel Renault was trying to pass a small Decauville when the two cars sideswiped and Renault lost control, spun out, and rolled over and into a tree. He died a few hours later. Another De Dietrich driver, an Englishman named Stead, was hit by a passing car which sliced off his front wheel and sent his car spinning into a ditch. Stead was thrown out and severely injured, while the car catapulted into the air above him and then landed over him like a bridge stretched across the ditch. One of the lady drivers in the race, Madame Du Gast, came along a few seconds later, stopped to pull Stead out from

under the wreckage, gave him first aid, and saw that he got into an ambulance.

But not all of the incidents which kept so many of the cars from getting through to Bordeaux were so gruesomely spectacular. Two of them involving Mercedes cars were almost comic. One of the best bets to win the Paris-Madrid was Camille Jenatzy, a red-bearded Belgian firebrand of a driver nicknamed "The Red Devil." Jenatzy was driving the latest 90 hp Mercedes, easily the most sophisticated car in the race, and burning up the road. Then, as an English motoring magazine called *The Car* said a few days after the race, "Jenatzy was making faster time than anyone else when the car mysteriously stopped and for three hours he endeavoured in vain to allocate the cause." Jenatzy suspected fuel pump problems or a clogged fuel line (a common ailment of the day) but it was not until his mechanic got to dismantling the carburetor that they found the cause, a mangled horsefly which had been sucked through the air intake and lodged in the jet. For want of a nail!

A French driver named Dergais was breezing along also on a Ninety Mercedes when suddenly the engine got temperamental and soon the big white car trickled off to the roadside and coughed to a stop. Dergais and his mechanic spent three and a half hours from crank handle to tailpipe and could find nothing. Then the frustrated Frenchman's eyes drifted toward a spare can behind the driver's seat. He picked it up and sniffed. "Ah, mon Dieu!" There was the answer—water. The Ninety Mercedes had a water-cooled brake system and the can had held a reserve supply for the water reservoir. In the heat of the race the mechanic had dumped it into the gas tank by mistake. Scratch one Mercedes.

In the early afternoon the lead cars began to crest a hill outside Bordeaux and then to collect in the impounding stock-

An "Edwardian XKE," the S.P.O. of 1908. Notice the canvas fenders.

THE MUSEUM OF AUTOMOBILES

ade to wait for the second stage of the race to Madrid the following day. As the cars pulled into the midway control, at first one at a time and then in clusters, a band played and thousands of spectators cheered and waved flags and handkerchiefs. But with the cars came the news of what was still happening back on the Paris-Bordeaux road, and the mood changed as if the sun had suddenly gone behind storm clouds.

At first the situation was complete confusion. Certainly not all of the stories could refer to *different* accidents. Then, as telegrams and late cars came in, officials pieced together the grisly story; 300 miles of death and destruction stretched across France. And if all this happened on the relatively good French roads, what could be expected tomorrow when the cars left for Spain? This time Monsieur Combes would not be persuaded or put off. "C'est tout, c'est fini!" was his irrevo-

Ford's sporty Model S of 1908.

THE MUSEUM OF AUTOMOBILES

cable reply. So, the Paris-Madrid which had begun with such spectacle and splendor ground to an inglorious halt at Bordeaux. So inglorious, in fact, that when a special train was made up to carry the cars back to Paris the drivers were not even permitted to start their engines and the cars were dragged to the railroad station in dusty disgrace behind teams of horses. It was a black hour for motor racing and the next day the newspapers reported it as "the motor massacre" and "the race to death."

Despite the debacle, there were two "winners" of the Paris-Madrid, in the heavy and light car classes. The first was won by Fernand Gabriel on a big racing Mors with a singularly magnificent piece of driving. Gabriel was launched from Versailles about in the middle of the field, perhaps the worst position of all. But he drove through the havoc and horror

De Dion Bouton of 1901, with tiller steering, vis-a-vis seating, and a wicker "picnic" basket behind.

THE MUSEUM OF AUTOMOBILES

with consummate skill—and uncanny luck—in five hours and fourteen minutes for an amazing 65-mph average, passing over seventy-five cars along the way. Gabriel's sheer daring was equalled by Louis Renault who pushed his little 30 hp at speeds up to 90 mph. Renault was the first driver to reach Bordeaux, but at the head of the column he knew nothing of the carnage behind him which included his brother Marcel among the dead.

Louis Renault's epic drive in his small car was more of the handwriting on the wall which Marcel had penned in the Paris-Vienna the year before: that a smaller car did not mean a slower car. This time, however, a few more people got the message. The influential English motoring paper *The Autocar* commented: "Nothing could be more surprising than the arrival of the Renault light carriage before the new high powered vehicles, for though it was by no means sure that Re-

Steering looks challenging on this 1898 Benz.

THE MUSEUM OF AUTOMOBILES

nault had won on time; it was obvious that the performance must be relatively better than that of the big cars of three times the nominal power. If the new Mercedes, Mors, and Panhards were unable to show a decided superiority over the light carriages on the magnificent Paris-Bordeaux (road) how would they expect to get an advantage on the Spanish roads where the light carriages would be more easily handled? *Already we have begun to see that from the point of autocar construction the race was likely to upset all the theories that have guided makers in the building of the high powered machines.*" When car designers began to think about that, the sports car climbed another rung on the ladder of motoring prestige.

The Paris-Madrid signaled the end of the colorful country-to-country races, with the exception of the New York to Paris of 1908 which was quite another matter. Yet the shock and public outrage were not really so deep as they might have been, considering that there was never anything in racing history to match the Paris-Madrid in devastation until the "Black Le Mans" of 1955 when eighty-five people died in a single accident. In fact, hardly a month had passed before the racers were back at it again, this time running the *Circuits des Ardennes* in Belgium. If the Paris-Madrid had been the end of a grand and reckless era, then perhaps the *Circuits des Ardennes* was the inkling of a new and saner one. The event was set up as a 300-mile race over a closed circuit of about fifty miles rather than through the free and open countryside. The Belgian army was out in force, but the sobered crowd they were to marshal presented few problems. A few drivers got banged about, but no one driving or watching was seriously hurt. The greatest hazard was the persistent bugaboo of all the early races, immense clouds of blinding and choking dust. A 70-hp Panhard driven by Baron Pierre de Crawhez was first in the heavy car class and a 60-hp Daraccq was the winner among light cars. The whole affair was quite civilized and responsible, and hopefully the shape of things to come in international motor sport.

The shape of things to come in cars was changing, too. In fact, elaborate ground work had already been laid even before the Paris-Madrid. By the turn of the century it was clear that the automobile was not only a *fait accompli* but also an invention of enormous potential although still in its pioneer era. Despite its undeveloped state and inevitable temper tantrums the automobile was becoming rapidly established for touring and business use. By Edwardian times an automobile was within the reach of the upper middle or professional class, and quite a few reached for them. Beyond the touring car was a developing, separate class of racing cars which had grown up with little regard for anything except speed and which were fairly useless for anything less than all-out racing. When someone combined these two virtues–practicality *and* performance–into one automobile, he would have the world's first sports car. In 1903 somebody did exactly that.

Chapter 3

THE SPORTS CAR IS BORN

It was a dissatisfied racing car owner rather than an inspired engineer who was at least partly responsible for the world's first real sports car. The unhappy customer was Emil Jellinek, a self-made Austrian *bon vivant* businessman whose adventuresome youth had taken him from the California gold fields to sweaty African plantations. By the gay nineties he had a flourishing import business bringing out-of-season African fruit to delicacy-conscious France. Jellinek settled graciously into the millionaire colony on the Riviera and got himself appointed as the Austro-Hungarian Consul General at Nice which gave him status, a coat full of medals, and a banquet room full of just the right friends for his perpetual speculations, investments, and financial ventures.

Jellinek was a canny businessman with an instinct for getting into the right thing at the right time. Lately, he had gotten interested in Gottlieb Daimler's motorcars and, once caught up in the thrills of speed, ordered, suggested, and then insisted upon better and faster cars. It was more than just a hobby; Jellinek built motoring into a status sport on the Riviera and became the chief purveyor of fast cars for his affluent friends.

F. Porsche, Austrian Daimler, Winner of Prince Henry Trophy

Austria Gets Prince Henry Trophy

BERLIN, June 9—Austria gets the famous Prince Henry trophy for keeps, the luck of the draw, which was held today to decide the final ownership of the big shield, favoring Ferdinand Porsche, chief engineer of the Austrian Daimler plant, who drove an Austrian Daimler to victory in this year's tour which was run this month. According to the deed of gift, the Prince Henry trophy had to be won twice by one concern to decide its ownership or, failing in this the three winners in the 3 years of running were to participate in the drawing which was to settle the problem. This drawing took place today and was participated in by Porsche, the 1910 winner, William Opel who won with an Opel in 1909, and Fritz Erle who drove the Benz to victory in 1908. Porsche drew the lucky number.

The results of this year's Prince Henry tour were cabled to Motor Age upon the completion of the contest, giving the standing of the first five cars. At the banquet tonight the report of the officials went more into detail, although the complete results have not as yet been compiled. As announced tonight the individual winner of the tour is Porsche, while second place has been awarded to Edward Fischer, a director of the Austrian Daimler Co., while Count Henrich Schonfeld was given third, thus ranking the Austrian Daimler one, two, three. Herbert Ephraim, driving an Opel and who made the fastest time in the speed trials was ranked fourth, while fifth place went to Fritz Erle, winner of the 1908 contest, who again drove a Benz. Those in the first twenty are five Austrian Daimlers, one Opel, seven Benz, four Mercedes, and a Presto, Alder and Gaggeneau.

Porsche won the second speed trial and was second to Fischer in the first one. This gave Porsche 20.90 plus percentage while Fischer had 20.51. Just how many cars really finished the tour is a mooted question, but is estimated that fully 25 per cent of the 121 contestants dropped out before the end of the tour.

Prince Henry made glad the hearts of the motorists tonight, when he announced that he had already offered a new trophy to the Kaiserlicher Automobile Club, and that negotiations were under way for a tour through England, one through Austria and another through Russia, the rulers of these countries being favorable to the idea.

The tour, which started from Berlin on June 2, finished at Hamburg on June 9. Of the 127 cars entered 121 started, the pacemaker being none other than Prince Henry himself. There was one woman contestant in the tour, Lilli Sternberg, who drove a four-cylinder Opel, and who has been a participant in all of the Prince Henry and Herkomer tours. The first day's run was to Braunschweig 154 1/0 miles, and included in the day's itinerary was the first of the two speed trials which was at a distance of 3.4 miles, each car being given 500 meters flying start. This test took place at Genthin and an official report of the result was as follows:

Contestant Car	Bore	Stroke	Time		Score
Erle, Benz	4.1	6.5	2:30	4-10	7.03
Fischer, Aus. Daimler	4.1	6.5	2:32		6.85
Ephraim, Opel	4.5	6.9	2:26		6.65
Paul, Adler	4.1	5.9	2:38		6.45
Gerber, Gaggenau	4.3	6.5	2:36		6.06
Opel, Opel	4.5	6.9	2:53	2-10	6.30
Spitzner, Benz	4.5	6.9	2:29	2-10	6.29
Lengerke, Bergman	4.1	6.5	2:39	2-10	6.09
Kidner, Vauxhall	3.5	4.7	3:30		4.40
Drebisel, Fiat	3.7	6.1	3:12		4.10
Trenbers, Dixi	2.95	4.7	3:45		3.91

Four Body Styles, Opel, Austrian Daimler, Benz and Mercedes

One of the Benz Cars in Prince Henry Tour

As will be noted by a reference to the table it will be seen that the fastest time was made by Ephraim in an Opel touring car who did the distance in 2:26, or at the rate of 83.8 miles per hour. However, under the formula, Ephraim was rated third, first place being given to Erle in the Benz. Outside of the speed trials there was nothing remarkable about the day's run, 114 of the cars making the night control within the time limit.

The second day's run was from Braunschweig to Cassel, a distance of 200 miles, which was a tiresome run because of the dust. The scenery, however, was beautiful. Many experienced tire troubles, while ignition troubles also bothered not a few. The third day out the tourists drove from Cassel to Nuremberg a distance of 207.7 miles. One of the Gaggeneaus had valve troubles and was withdrawn. An Opel broke a differential, and a Stoewer broke a crankshaft pin. On this day also tire troubles were frequent.

Sunday was spent in Nuremberg and the 400 participants in the tour enjoyed a day of rest. The officials, however, had no such leisure and spent the day listening to complaints. As a result of the deliberation E. Leuschner, driver of a Protos,

Resume of the Big German Tour

was disqualified because of an accident in which a girl was injured. Although it was proven that the driver was not responsible for the accident, the rules made disqualification compulsory. At this stage there still were 108 cars in the tour. No. 35 Benz had been withdrawn on account of losing a motor bearing; Nos. 39 and 42, both Bergmann Metallurgiques, had been withdrawn because of having been burned; No. 87 Mercedes was out because of motor bearing troubles; No. 92 Fiat on account of valve troubles; No. 98 Brennabor on account of a broken crankshaft pin; No. 22 Gaggeneau on account of a broken piston; No. 68 Opel on account of a broken differential; No. 111 Mathis on account of valve troubles; No. 113 Mathis on account of a motor bearing; No. 115 Stoewer on account of motor bearing troubles; while No. 72 Protos was disqualified by the officials of the tour.

The run from Nuremberg to Strasburg the fourth day's running, was the longest of the tour, the distance 221.4 miles, the roads being dusty and the sun exceedingly hot. The day's run was marred by an accident to Buchroh's Opel which hit a stone, breaking a wheel and smashing the radiator. Reichstein's Brennabor caught fire and was wrecked, while others who experienced trouble were a Fiat with a crankshaft, an Austrian Daimler with a broken spring, and two Stoewers with motor troubles.

The second speed trial was held during the run between Strasburg and Metz. The distance of the trial was 3.4 miles, the same as the first one, the course being near Heiligkruz. The trials were marred by a double fatality when a tire on the Adler driven by Franz Heine blew up, causing the car to run into a tree, killing the observer and mechanic. This delayed the trial an hour. While no official results have been given out as yet regarding the results of this trial, it is unofficially stated that the best time of the day was made by Von Jagerneyer in an Austrian Daimler who did 2:22.4 which however did not make him the winner under the formula. Porsche in the Aus-

Two Views of the Austrian Daimler Motor Used by Winner

His effect on Daimler's was catalytic. The story of his midwifery in creating the Mercedes and getting it named for his ten-year-old daughter is one of the most famous in motor lore and needs no repetition here. The original 1901 Mercedes which emerged as a result of Jellinek's relentless proddings has been called the world's first modern car and featured such innovations as a pressed Krupp steel frame, coil spring clutch, improved brakes, efficient honeycomb radiator, and a marvelously efficient engine which began to lean away from displacement in favor of refinement. Yet, it was that car's successor, the great "Sixty" of 1903, which is generally recognized as the world's first true sports car.

The Sixty Mercedes reversed the philosophy that better touring cars are developed from successful competition cars. The Sixty was, in fact, developed out of a large 9.2-litre, 60-hp Daimler touring car which Chief Engineer Wilhelm Maybach had lightened by two hundred pounds. He then fitted the new Mercedes with further refinements such as better suspension, improved starter and electrical system, an even more efficient honeycomb radiator, a primitive but effective system of water-cooled brakes, and interchangeable sprockets to match ratios to sporting or touring requirements. Paul Meyan, the president of the Automobile Club de France, had the privilege of visiting the Daimler plant as the new Sixties were in production and was impressed with what he saw. His impressions were carried in *La France Automobile* and were picked up and reprinted in the English paper *The Autocar* in November of 1902:

"Judging from the bare indications published in *La France*

The Prince Henry of Prussia Competition in the days before World War I was big news in the automotive world. Here, a "Résumé of the Big German Tour" and an account of the 1-2-3 victory of Ferdinand Porsche's Austro-Daimler sports cars was cabled across the Atlantic to the magazine "Motor Age" for interested American readers.

SMITHSONIAN INSTITUTION

Automobile, we are likely to see some noteworthy improvements in the new type of Mercedes cars which will be making their first public appearance at the Nice meeting in March next. Having visited the Cannstatt works, Mr. Paul Meyan is greatly struck with what he has seen, and only regrets that he is not permitted to describe fully the many ingenious devices that are destined once more to make the Mercedes one of the most interesting vehicles of the year. The weight of the frame, springs, and axles has been further reduced by 220 pounds, and at the same time their solidity and rigidity have been increased. Armoured wood construction has given way to steel, and the frame members are stamped out of sheet steel U-shape, the weight being only 77 pounds. This is also the weight of the rear axle, which is forged with a double-T section. The cooling surface of the radiator has been doubled by a new method of arranging the tubes without increasing

Just before the 1903 Gordon Bennett a fire destroyed the entire Mercedes team of cars and an American sportsman named Clarence Gray Dinsmore offered his Sixty Mercedes to the company. It was race-prepared for Belgian driver Camille Jenatzy who drove it to a classic victory through the Irish countryside.

DAIMLER-BENZ A.G.

the volume. There are many new features about the motor, which will have a double system of ignition, if required, the one being the usual magneto and the other, apparently, a dynamo without accumulators. The magneto is situated in front of the motor where it is easily accessible. . . . For the cars to be sent to Nice, the motors will have a bore of 170 mm and a stroke of 140 mm, and will run at from 1000 to 1200 revolutions. In view of the big demand for Mercedes cars, the company are (sic) making preparations for considerably increasing their productive capacity, and instead of building fifteen cars a month, as at present, they will soon be able to turn out forty."

What Wilhelm Maybach had really created in the Sixty Mercedes—technical jargon aside—was one of those rare blendings of form and function which makes a true classic outlive its mere utility value, whether it is an automobile, a fine rifle, architecture, or a piece of furniture. The Sixty was not only the ultimate expression of the state of the automotive arts in 1903 but also a beautiful machine.

The Sixty Mercedes was equally at home blasting over a race course at more than a mile a minute or tooling leisurely along a country road in April, so great was its flexibility. The formula had been met: performance plus practicality equals sports car. Like its ancestral Mercedes of 1901, the car could even be fitted with a second seat behind the driver and passenger and with a folding top to complete the conversion to a practical touring car. As no single automobile had ever done before, the Sixty captured the imagination of drivers all over the world. Of course, Emil Jellinek had a Mercedes at the Nice Week competition that year, but it was overshadowed by another Sixty brought from Germany by an English sportsman named Alfred Harmsworth which recorded the fastest time in the speed trials, an amazing 74.3 mph. Harmsworth, later Lord Northcliffe, loved the car so much that he would never part with it even long after it was technically obsolete, and eventually it became a family heirloom. Still Harmsworth-owned, this pristinely restored example of one of the earliest

James Gordon Bennett advanced the cause of pioneer motor sport with a series of international races and commissioned this magnificent silver trophy for the victor. Bennett himself never attended a single one of his races.

AUTOMOBILE CLUB DE FRANCE

Sixties stands in Lord Montagu's Motor Museum at Beaulieu in Brockenhurst, England.

Another early and volatilely enthusiastic Sixty owner was a young Italian nobleman and grape grower named Vincenzo Florio who was so enthralled by automobiles generally and the new Mercedes in particular that he organized a new race—the Coppa Florio—to be run near Brescia, and promptly entered his own car. The race was a success, although try as he might Florio never managed to win it. Three years later Vincenzo Florio organized another race for sports cars which has gone down into legend as perhaps the ruggedest race ever run, the rough and rather infamous Targa Florio. As if the inhospitable Sicilian mountain course were not enough of a challenge, drivers were reporting that in practice runs the local banditi found the new-fangled automobiles wonderful for moving target practice. Florio solved the problem with that marvelously Italian grasp of the logic of life. He made the bandit leaders official race stewards, with appropriate ceremonial trappings, so it now became a matter of honor for them to leave the cars unmolested. This did not, however, even in much later races prevent patriotic spectators from giving wrong directions and signals to disoriented non-Italian drivers.

The fame of the new Mercedes shortly spanned the Atlantic and a number of wealthy Americans such as William K. Vanderbilt, Foxhall Keene, and Clarence Gray Dinsmore bought the German sports cars. Vanderbilt had been a customer of Daimler's since their first high performance car, the Phoenix of 1899, and he enjoyed driving fast cars on the good roads of Long Island. After a while his passion condensed into the Vanderbilt Cup races which were run from 1904 to 1916, first on Long Island and later in Wisconsin, Georgia, and California. For a time, the sight of "Willie K." Vanderbilt behind the wheel of a big white Mercedes burning up the roads of Long Island was the image of an era.

Dinsmore was an equally ardent aficionado of the race and perhaps his greatest contribution to the sport was having his Sixty Mercedes in the right place at the right time. The Daimler company had entered five of their enlarged 90-hp cars in the Gordon Bennett race scheduled for July of 1903, but these and about seventy other cars were destroyed in a fire on June 10th which completely leveled the Daimler works at Cannstatt. Two other privately entered Sixties were to be driven by Foxhall Keene and Baron De Caters, but no works entry survived. So, Dinsmore stepped in and offered his sporting Sixty to the Daimler company which stripped it down and prepared it for racing as best they could for crack driver Cammile Jenatzy to do battle in the Gordon Bennett race.

A bit of background for the Gordon Bennett is worth a small digression here. Beginning in 1900 James Gordon Bennett, the American newspaper publisher, sponsored a series of great international automobile races and commissioned a magnificent silver trophy called the *Coupe Internationale* to be created. In 1902 the Bennett race was run concurrently with a part of the Paris-Vienna; the Bennett portion from Paris to

Jules Goux poses after victory in the Coupe de Catalogne Voiturettes in Spain in 1909 with one of the very successful long-stroke voiturettes.

AUTOMOBILES PEUGEOT

Innsbruck. A dark horse, an English Napier driven by Selwyn Edge, won the Bennett trophy and so, under the rules of the contest, England was supposed to be the host nation for the following year's race. But rules or no there was a strong anti-automobile sentiment still afoot in England which was not about to let the "motorcar menace" loose to race on English roads. Some such sentiment was lodged in Parliament; mostly, as might be expected, in the House of Commons. The "British Gordon Bennett" came at a time when one member in Commons named Watson rose to complain that "he had nearly been knocked down by a motor at the entrance of the House of Commons," and "hoped that means would be adopted

75 hp FIAT of 1904 burning up the road from Brescia to Cremona. FIAT fielded some interesting and successful sports-racers from 1900 to 1927.

FIAT

PALME
ÉCONOMIE · DURÉ

for catching, upsetting, and smashing up these destructive wretches, who have no more regard for human life than if they were flies." Similar un-English propensities toward violence could even be found among the sporting aristocracy: the Marquis of Queensbury advocated that speeding motorcars should be "shot on sight."

The Paris-Madrid, of course, provided Mr. Watson and his friends with a fresh stock of ammunition. But, since a measure of English international prestige and flag-showing was on the block, a compromise was arranged so that the race could be held near Ballyshannon, Ireland. Despite the Mercedes misfortune and the legal complications, the 1903 Gordon Bennett turned out to be one of the great races of the classic era. For one thing, it was one of the most genuinely international races, with three German, three British, three French, and three American entries—the very embodiment of Mr. Bennett's spirit of internationalism. The American presence consisted of a pair of Wintons, one a whopping 17 litre, which demonstrated that the American love of big engines came early, and a Peerless brought over and driven by the company president Louis P. Mooers. The Peerless lasted only a single lap, but later the car was to redeem itself back home as the famous Peerless "Green Dragon" with cigar-chewing Barney Oldfield behind the wheel. Perhaps on race day it was unhappy with its coat of red paint, which was then the American racing color. The logical idea of a separate racing color for each nation is attributed to Count Eliot Zborowski, and by the time of the 1903 Gordon Bennett France had blue, Germany had white, England had green, and the United States had red, which was later given to the Italians when the Americans ceased to be serious participants in European racing.

The "Irish" Gordon Bennett was a 327½ mile race laid out

Styles in competition cars had begun to change. An early aerodynamic "boat tail" Peugeot takes a corner in the "Meeting de Boulogne" in 1911.

AUTOMOBILES PEUGEOT

over two circuits of roughly 40 miles and 52 miles each between Ballyshannon and Kilcullen. With the Paris-Madrid fresh in mind, the Irish viceroy drafted so many policemen from all over the country that Ireland must have had precious little police protection elsewhere that day, but at least it had a casualty-free Gordon Bennett and a robustly Irish good time. As defender of the title, Selwyn Edge was first away at 7:00 A.M. sharp, followed by the eleven other cars at seven minute intervals. Along with Mooers' Peerless, dropouts began to pile up from the first lap. Edge's companion Napier, driven by J. W. Stocks, went off the road and through a fence, Charles Jarrott had a spectacular but fairly harmless crash, and Foxhall Keene bent the rear axle of his Sixty all within the

A trio of Lion-Peugeot voiturettes posed at the 1909 *Course des Voiturettes.*

AUTOMOBILES PEUGEOT

first four laps. As American hopes evaporated and British chances dwindled while Edge continued to fall back with tire troubles, a duel between Camille Jenatzy on his borrowed Sixty and the Chevalier René de Knyff with his 13.7-litre Panhard developed. It was de Knyff's belief that a combination of his car and skill (he had been racing since 1896) would ultimately give him an edge over everyone except Jenatzy, whom he expected to burn himself out long before the finish.

With somewhat better communication between driver and team about Jenatzy's position, de Knyff could have won. But he held back too long and realized too late that the combination of Jenatzy's daring, a Mercedes Sixty, and perhaps a dash of Irish luck was just too much. On the last lap, the Chevalier drove like mad but nothing he could do would dissolve those eleven minutes that still separated him from Jenatzy at the finish. The flamboyant red-bearded Belgian had driven a brilliant race at speeds up to 85 mph over narrow

A heated moment during the Circuit de Provence, 1907.

AUTOMOBILES PEUGEOT

country roads conceived for Irish jaunting carts, and he had done it with a stripped down sports car pitted against big displacement, all-out racing cars.

Although it lacked something of the cachet and it yielded somewhat to the temptation to escalate displacement, the Sixty's successor—the twelve-litre Ninety—continued in production until the First World War. Yet even well before that there were signs of obsolescence in such cars. Other men were at work on cars that would represent the link between the pioneer sports cars of Paris-Madrid and Gordon Bennett days and the epic sports machines that would blossom in the years after the war. One such man was Ferdinand Porsche, who had worked under and learned from the Wilhelm Maybach tra-

A Peugeot checks in at a control along the route of a 1905 race in Alsace.

AUTOMOBILES PEUGEOT

Classic motorsport; a Peugeot voiturette at speed in 1905.
AUTOMOBILES PEUGEOT

dition of the Mercedes Sixty but was determined not to emulate it.

When he came to the Austro-Daimler Motor Company in Weiner-Neustatt, Austria, in 1906 as a young engineer, Ferdinand Porsche already had a varied and successful career in creating cars, including a royal electric limousine that was the delight of the Austrian Emperor Franz Josef and that still survives in a Viennese museum. So, Porsche did not come to *Osterreichische-Daimler*, or Austro-Daimler, quite hat-in-hand as the classic young job seeker looking for a junior niche in the company. Old Gottlieb Daimler's son Paul was Chief Engineer and was just about to return to the parent company's new plant at Stuttgart when Porsche showed up. Both the timing and the talent were right, and Porsche started out

5

at the top of the ladder as Chief Engineer, which certainly must have been a boost to the self-confidence of a thirty-year-old guy in a culture which worshipped age and experience more than youthful enthusiasm.

Austro-Daimler was the Austrian branch of the *Daimler Motoren Gesellschaft*, but it maintained only a fairly casual relationship with its parent company. In time, the two even drew apart in design and marketed rather dissimilar cars. If the difference did not begin with Porsche, it certainly accelerated when he sat down behind the drawing boards at Weiner-Neustatt. His first project was a "high performance touring car" to compete in the *Kaiserpreis* of 1907. This was an event inaugurated by Kaiser Wilhelm II—who rather liked cars—and called for a then modest displacement limit of eight litres and set up other specifications for what clearly amounted to sports cars rather than pure racing machines. The true sports car was coming of age.

Porsche did not start with a completely new car, but took a standard 45-hp Mercedes chassis and began modifying it to suit himself. First, he stripped off the standard gearbox and rear-end assembly and fitted an electric motor into the rear as part of his multi-ratio and highly variable electric transmission. The idea was ingenious, but it was somewhat ahead of its time and technology and required heavy, complex parts. The finished car, called the Mercedes-Mixte, failed to qualify for the well-attended *Kaiserpreis*, which had attracted about eighty entries distilled from two elimination races.

The Mercedes-Mixte was not one of the triumphs of Porsche's long and brilliant career, but it was characteristic of the unconventionality of a man who would one day design

Ferdinand Porsche himself at the wheel of his victorious Austro-Daimler 27/80 "Prince Henry Model" at the 1910 Prince Henry of Prussia competition. The car's great strength was its advanced 5.7-litre, overhead-cam, inclined-valve engine which could develop up to 100 hp with great efficiency.

DAIMLER-BENZ A.G.

The famous Benz driver Fritz Erle at the wheel of the Benz entry in the 1908 Prince Henry Tour.

DAIMLER-BENZ A.G.

Willie Poege at the wheel of a Benz in the 1911 Prince Henry Tour which was run partly in Germany and partly in England that year.

DAIMLER-BENZ A.G.

such diverse machines as supercharged Mercedes sports cars, quixotic rear-engined Auto-Union Grand Prix racers, the fearsome Tiger Tank—and, of course, the Volkswagen. On his next try, however, he looked to something a little more "conventionally unconventional" and returned to ordinary means of transmitting power to the rear wheels.

The *Kaiserpreis* signaled a trend toward genuine sports car events for amateur drivers, and the enthusiasm was shared by the Kaiser's brother, Prince Henry of Prussia, who organized the "Prince Henry of Prussia Competition" and offered a big Teutonic shield as trophy. The event was composed of speed and reliability trials as well as a sort of grand tour and rally laced with fun and games at the great houses of wealthy sportsmen along the way. Even a half century later the idea sounds inviting, but now, sadly, it is impractical because of automotive overpopulation. The publicity and sales value of winning the Prince Henry was enormous because of the similarity of the cars to standard production models, and Austro-Daimler, along with a number of other companies, was willing to invest in an all-out new car to win it. Ferdinand Porsche created it.

The car that Porsche responded with became the first really famous one in his long line of successes. The completed car, known officially as the 27/80 Austro-Daimler "Prince Henry Model," had a striking aerodynamic design and a certain essential, elemental elegance about it. Appearance aside, the machine's strength lay in its magnificent 5.7-litre, four-cylinder, overhead-camshaft, inclined-valve engine which could turn out up to 100 hp with high efficiency. It was a lively and responsive machine that clearly advanced the cause of the sports car a giant step. How much it moved sports cars forward can be seen in comparison with the Sixty Mercedes, which required 9.2 litres to produce its peak 60 hp, while the new Austro-Daimler put out 40 percent more power with not much over half of the Sixty's displacement.

The Prince Henry tour for 1910 began on June 2nd at Berlin, rambled across Germany at an average of about 200

miles a day, and ended in Hamburg on the 9th. It seems a civilized, leisurely sort of motor sport, far removed from the pressure and pace of something like the Paris-Vienna or Paris-Madrid, but not entirely removed from danger. Speeds ranged up to about 84 mph, and on the last day a German Adler blew a tire and skidded out of control into a tree, killing the official observer in the car and the mechanic.

If the Austro-Daimler company still harbored any doubts about Ferdinand Porsche as their Chief Engineer they should have been fully resolved by the time the cars reached the German coast. Although Fritz Erle on a Benz had taken honors in the speed trials and Pomeroy's Vauxhalls had attracted a lot of attention and admiration, it was clear that Porsche's Austro-Daimlers were the stars of the show. Porsche himself drove in the Prince Henry Competition and he took first place, followed by Edward Fischer, an Austro-Daimler director, second, and Count Heinrich Schonfeld, third. A clean win-place-show sweep for Austro-Daimler. And even after the engines had cooled, the Porsche luck held that day. The rules provided that if one maker won the competition for two consecutive years he got to keep the shield-trophy. Fritz Erle had won for Benz in 1908 and Wilhelm Opel for Opel in 1909 and so it was decided that the permanent holder of the trophy would be drawn by lot from among Erle, Opel, and Porsche. After the victory banquet the shield went home to Weiner-Neustatt.

Those days of the *Kaiserpreis*, Prince Henry, and Herkomer tours just before World War I were exciting ones for the emerging sports car, and the drama of discovery was also being played out in places far from Ferdinand Porsche's Alpine drawing office. From England a young designer named Laurence Pomeroy brought over a car to run in the Prince Henry of 1910 and learned some valuable lessons about what

Benz driver Fritz Erle chats with Prince Henry of Prussia in Vienna during the 1909 competition.

DAIMLER-BENZ A.G.

Lord Northcliffe's Sixty Mercedes, now preserved at the Montagu Motor Museum, is one of the oldest Sixties and was one of the fastest, recording 74.3 mph in the trials at Nice in 1903.

MONTAGU MOTOR MUSEUM

sports cars were going to be. In Spain, a Swiss engineer switched from locomotives to motorcars and came up with a sports car that charmed a king. In Alsace-Lorraine, an individualistic Italian genius was beginning a career which would produce perhaps the king of sports cars. And in America, the Stutz "Bearcat" and Mercer "Raceabout" were battling each other on the road and in the public imagination to show Americans what sports cars were all about.

Chapter 4

THE STOIC SKYROCKET

"Lord Hovenden detached from his motorcar was an entirely different being from the Lord Hovenden who lounged with such a deceptive air of languor behind the steering wheel of a Vauxhall Velox. Half an hour spent in the roaring wind of his own speed transformed him from a shy and diffident boy into a cool-headed hero, daring not merely in the affairs of the road, but in the affairs of life as well. The fierce wind blew away his diffidence; the speed intoxicated him out of his self-consciousness."*

In these lines from *Those Barren Leaves,* Aldous Huxley captured the notion that a car can be more than merely an assembly of metal parts. He found that a certain kind of car can be symbolic, or even mystic, a civilized totem which could change a man's personality from mild to masterful. The car Huxley chose for the transformation was appropriately a Vauxhall 30/98, a hearty and historic English sports car of the middle twenties which traced its ancestry directly back to the Prince Henry competition.

* Used with permission, Harper & Bros., New York, N.Y.

The early Vauxhalls form an important link in the development of the sports car. They started in a rather odd way, partly as a result of a young engineering student's private war with the French language. French was certainly not the forte of a promising young Englishman named Laurence H. Pomeroy and when a professor suggested that he read French books for a friendlier footing in the language he saw no reason why they shouldn't be about his favorite subject, automobiles. French automotive books were not hard to find, and one in particular on Monsieur Hierman's theories of increased engine efficiency provided more than grammar lessons.

Passing both his technical and his language exams, Pomeroy came to work for the Vauxhall Company at Luton in 1905. Vauxhall was an interesting, typically English organization founded in the middle 1800s by a Scotsman named Alexander Wilson as the "Vauxhall Iron Works." Its specialty was building marine engines. In the late 1890s it took notice of the new motorcar and a company engineer named Hodges ran up a few experimental engines for automobiles, one of them amazingly a radial design. In the summer of 1903 the first Vauxhall was offered for sale. Even though it was a first venture the original Vauxhall was a thoroughly thought out little car; simply built, durable, and highly reliable by the standards of the day. The little 5-hp, single-cylinder car was perhaps a bit old fashioned with its dated tiller steering but a good buy at £150 and it was warmly received. One doctor-owner wrote to a motoring magazine about his experiences with a new Vauxhall: "The wear and tear of driving at fifteen miles per hour is, in my opinion, of almost negligible quality. The average cost of running has worked out to one third of the upkeep of my horse. I have at present never experienced a moment's worry on the road. An inexpensive, reliable, and comfortable means of locomotion, say I." The next year brought the refinements of a reverse gear, steering wheel, wood-spoked artillery wheels, and one extra horsepower. The price stayed the same.

In the year that Laurence Pomeroy came to Luton the

The first Vauxhall, which appeared in the summer of 1903. The car was powered by a single-cylinder, 5 hp, horizontally mounted engine with chain drive. There was coil spring suspension all around, but only two forward gears. The next year's version brought a steering wheel, reverse gear, and one extra horsepower. About forty of these original Vauxhalls were built; only two survive.

GENERAL MOTORS OVERSEAS OPERATIONS

company was building one of its most unusual, if least successful, models. At the suggestion of the Earl of Ranfurly they had married the motorcar to the hansom cab and came up with a bizarre offspring that placed the motor forward and the cab driver in his traditional spot above and behind the passengers with a view over their heads. The Vauxhall hansom cab fell between both worlds of the horse and motor fans, and apparently neither one of them liked it very much and few were made. Yet it was a fascinating, perhaps unique, creation and if any survive today they must indeed be dear to their owners.

That was the sort of company to which the ambitious young Pomeroy came in 1905: a firm whose approach to the motor car was based on conservative ideas to sell at reasonable prices, a firm that was not shy about even retreating to a motorized horse cab. It did not seem to be a very encouraging climate for Pomeroy's thoughts about exciting high performance equipment. The company sold 76 cars in 1904, and that year added to its line a 12/14-hp, three-cylinder car which sold for £375 (about $1875), fully equipped. The following year a four-cylinder model was introduced and was in production when Pomeroy arrived.

Pomeroy's first assignment at Vauxhall was to work on an improved four-cylinder, live-axle car of 12/16 hp, which went into production and sold for £417, complete. The young designer's maiden project turned out well and, in a rare burst of enthusiasm, the company entered a car in the Scottish Reliability Trials of 1907. Pomeroy's first Vauxhall was entered in Class III for cars with a chassis price of from £300 to £400. Among its immediate competitors it was the fourth cheapest car, but in horsepower it ranked eleventh in a field of fourteen. All things considered—including the sea of mud and rugged Scottish terrain in which the Trials were held—the Vauxhall accounted for itself moderately well. On reliability for "involuntary stoppages" it was rated fourth in its class, receiving two marks deducted for "adjusting accelerator rod." The car earned 85.9 marks out of a possible 100 under "weights and (fuel) consumption performances," and finished seventh in the hill climb results, which was not discouraging in view of its low horsepower output.

It is unlikely that a twenty-six-year-old novice engineer had much authority in the affairs of the company, yet contemporary with Pomeroy's coming the firm began to shake off its old conservatism. A separate company called "Vauxhall Motors, Ltd." was set up in 1906 and began to quicken with the times. Preoccupied perhaps, the company belatedly

"C-Type" Vauxhall with designer Laurence Pomeroy at the wheel. The "C-Type" of early 1910 was the immediate ancestor of the epic "Prince Henry" Vauxhall. Pomeroy and his car were posed at Lynmouth, Devon near the site of the Lynton Hill Climb.
GENERAL MOTORS OVERSEAS OPERATIONS

The Prince Henry Vauxhall, a memorable milestone in the development of the sports car, quickly became the "in car" for the Edwardian English sporting set.

GENERAL MOTORS OVERSEAS OPERATIONS

decided to enter the 1908 Scottish Trials, only to find that its chief engineer was off in Egypt recuperating from an illness. The logical thing to do was to turn to Pomeroy, and the directors dumped the whole project in his lap.

They were not to be disappointed. Recalling Hierman's theories of high compression and enlarged valve area, Pomeroy looked creatively at the still prosaic side-valve engine and did some mental sketching. The final results were that he doubled the rated horsepower while staying within the original three-litre displacement. Things could get a bit hairy if the engine were kept at full throttle at its (for then) high speed of 2400 rpm, but the lively machine did go as advertised and the directors were delighted. The two-thousand-mile run in the Scottish Reliability Trials was even more than Pomeroy's youthful enthusiasm could hope for. Nothing in its class could lay a hand on the new Vauxhall in the hill climb; it was well over half a minute in front of its nearest competitor. There was not a single unscheduled stop in the distance run, and in the "weight and consumption performances" the car returned an average of twenty-six miles to the (imperial) gallon. After the Trials a motoring journal noted that such astonishing performance from a virtually untested car "drew Vauxhall from a comparatively uninteresting background into the full glare of public interest."

The showing in the Scottish Trials also drew some of the company's management out of their offices and behind the wheels of new sporting Vauxhalls. The Trials had, in effect, been something of a primeval sports car rally and two knowledgeable English commentators, Cecil Clutton and John Stanford, in their book *The Vintage Motorcar* (B. T. Batsford, Ltd., London, 1954), maintain that the event "gave birth to the sports car." At any rate, the company directors enjoyed piloting their product in competition as well as watching the happy effects of victory on-sales. Competition was now company policy, and over the next few years Laurence Pomeroy

Vauxhall was overshadowed by Ferdinand Porsche's Austro-Daimlers at the Prince Henry of Prussia Trials, but offered fast (72 mph) and reliable performance. Here, a Prince Henry Vauxhall on the road with a German officer on board as official observer.

GENERAL MOTORS OVERSEAS OPERATIONS

became a popular, and busy, man around the Vauxhall works.

Speed records were another approach to notoriety and a lightened single seat version of Pomeroy's car hit 88.8 mph and later with further development topped 100 mph. Since Vauxhall was establishing itself as a sports car builder, it was only natural that the company should be interested in the first Prince Henry of Prussia competition run in 1910. Pomeroy set to work on a revised sporting version of his successful "Twenty" and three of the new cars were sent off to the wars with fanfare and expectation. The fanfare that year of course went to Ferdinand Porsche and his winning Austro-Daimlers, but even though formal victory eluded him Pomeroy created a milestone in the history of the sports car.

The "Prince Henry" Vauxhall contained all of Pomeroy's current engineering expertise, but perhaps its greatest asset was its appearance. It was a stark, essential looking four-seater with a striking, almost arrogant, V-nose radiator which seemed to be half smiling and half snarling. In 1904 a long traditional Vauxhall trademark appeared, the characteristic "Vauxhall flutes," which began at the radiator and continued back across the hood to the cowl. The style was used on the Prince Henry, and it was about the car's only concession to ornament. It was a graceful effect, not unlike the fluting on a piece of Adams architecture. When the production model of the Prince Henry Vauxhall was first put on display at the Olympia Motor Show in 1911, it attracted a great deal of attention as the first standard production English sports car, although that term did not come into use for another decade or so. At £485 the car was moderately priced for the high performance and style which it offered, and the new Prince Henry Vauxhall quickly became the car to be seen in for the English sporting set. In fact, it was even seen as far off as Russia and was very successful there in races run under the Czar's patronage. Czar Nicholas II was impressed by the swift little English cars and ordered a long-wheelbase, 35-hp, six-cylinder formal Vauxhall with tasseled window blinds, wire wheels, and pure white rubber tires.

Interest continued to grow in the Prince Henry Vauxhall as it collected victories and as Pomeroy continued to improve it. In 1912 he increased engine size from three to four litres, with bore and stroke of 95 x 140 mm, which now gave about 75 hp. The following year a bigger chassis with a 130-inch wheelbase appeared. This combination earned another world's record for a speed endurance run of 91.5 mph for five hours.

By 1913 England had become very car minded, particularly about sporting machines. One of the favorite gathering places for drivers was the Shelsley Walsh hill climb near Worcester, an ideal place to settle gentlemanly disagreements over the merits of particular cars. Although only 1143 yards long, it was a demanding run with a double curve near the center and an average gradient of 1 in 9.35. That is, for every 9.35 feet, the road rose one foot. A gentleman named A. Joseph Higgenson from Stockport had his eye on the hill record, which at the time was held by a man named Holder, who had done the run in 62.2 seconds. One day in March 1913, Mr. Higgenson came down to Luton and calmly asked for a car which would unseat Mr. Holder at the next Shelsley Walsh, seemingly unmindful that it was but thirteen weeks away. Higgenson was told that Vauxhall Motors, Ltd. and Mr. Pomeroy would see what could be done. What was done made sports car history and opened a new era for Vauxhall.

What was delivered to Higgenson was a stock 4-litre Prince Henry with the engine bored out to 4.5 litres and mounted under a slender, doorless four-seater body made of aluminum. The trademark Vauxhall flutes were still there in the gleaming bonnet, but the Vee radiator was gone, replaced by a businesslike flat one. The flat radiator perhaps gave the car a more prosaic look but Higgenson was hardly concerned about that. His concern was raised, however, when on his first run over the dry and crumbly roadbed of Shelsley Walsh the car gave him a high 70 seconds. On the second run he beat Holder's 62.2 with a 58, only to have another driver follow him with a fractionally lower score. Calmly, he had at it for the third time and finished in 55.2 seconds, a score which stood for the next fifteen years! While Higgenson's special appeared perhaps a little stoic next to the endearing old Prince Henry, Vauxhall realized that they had a skyrocket on their hands. When the same car lapped Brooklands track at an average 108 mph, they were sure of it.

The factory built a duplicate of Higgenson's special car and both were run in most available events. This new car, which had been developed out of the Prince Henry, might well have been called the "Thirteen," for the first had been built in just thirteen weeks, in 1913, and in the next year of racing the two cars won thirteen first places and thirteen seconds. Actually, the name by which the car became famous—the 30/98 Vauxhall—is still an unsolved mystery. Supposedly, an unknown technician named the car, but his method is obscure because neither figure represents either the RAC horsepower rating (23.8) or the brake horsepower (90). Nevertheless, the name stuck for the car's thirteen-year production span, one more "thirteen." The 30/98 was still mostly an experiment when World War I intervened. Five had been built in 1913, Vauxhall's most rewarding year in competition, seven were made in 1914, and one in 1915; a total of *thirteen.*

In December, 1919 the 30/98 was offered to the public on a regular production basis. The price had gone up stiffly from the days of the £485 Prince Henry to £1665 for a sports/touring version of the 30/98. To say that the car was received well would be an understatement because it became one of the most successful and best loved sports cars ever built in Britain. The reasons for its sporting success and the still enduring English reverence for a car that hasn't been built since 1926 are sometimes obscure to Americans. Part of the answer may lie in the fact that the 30/98 was built *for* Englishmen, well before the "export market" philosophy evolved in ear-

A Prince Henry chassis fitted with racing body with wasp tail and gracefully flared mudguards. Date is 1912–13, and the works driver A. J. Hancock is at the wheel.

GENERAL MOTORS OVERSEAS OPERATIONS

13

nest. For England, the 30/98 was a happy combination of the right thing at the right time. There was in England at the time a reasonably affluent middle class with quite as much sporting blood as the peers of the realm, if sometimes a bit less cash. The imbalance between taste and resources was met by the 30/98, which, while certainly not an economy car, could deliver the verve and vigor of cars costing much more. The visual image of the 30/98 also tends to baffle modern Americans because the "Velox" sports/touring version would seem to look more at home with somebody's Aunt Agatha at the wheel than screeching around the curves on Shelsley Walsh hill. Yet, despite the passage of half a century, the car still has a no-nonsense sensuality about it that quietly lets you know it means business.

Under the hood, the 30/98 seemed equally ordinary, even to the point of making you wonder what made it go the way it did. The four-cylinder, 4.5-litre engine was no forecast of the future; a simply designed sidevalve engine hardly more impressive than Henry Ford's Model A (although rather better finished). But the lessons that Laurence Pomeroy had learned about compression and adequate valve area were matched by meticulous machining that produced a powerful, high-revving engine. The secret of Vauxhall success on the road was not unlike the "secret" of Sir Henry Royce, who rarely innovated in the usual sense, but preferred to rely upon basic and proven designs and to refine them to perfection with near-fanatical attention to detail. The critic who called the Rolls-Royce "a triumph of workmanship over design" was also on the right track toward describing the Vauxhall 30/98.

Also like Rolls-Royce, Vauxhall incorporated improvements into the 30/98 whenever the engineers were sure they were worthwhile. Some notable changes came in 1922 with the new OE 30/98. The stroke was shortened from 150 to 140 mm and overhead pushrod-operated valves were added. This increased the efficiency of the engine, revving it up from 2800 to 3500 rpm and upping horsepower from 90 to 112. Front wheel brakes were added the same year, and the top gear ratio was altered from 3:1 to 3.3:1. In 1926 a counterbalanced crankshaft was added. All of this was obvious improvement, but curiously, none of the cars enjoying it was able to top the records set by the 30/98 when it was built to satisfy Mr. Higgenson.

The Vauxhall "arms," a crest in the form of a mythical wyvern borrowed from a colorful rogue of Magna Carta days named Fulk le Breant, were further honored between 1920 and 1923 (when Vauxhall retired from competition) with 75 wins, 52 seconds, 35 third places, and 14 hill climb records. Endurance runs were equally fruitful. A 30/98 covered 445 miles of South African road in 10 hours and 56 minutes, and another raced across Australia to cover the 643 miles between Sydney and Brisbane in 18 hours and 43 minutes.

A historic moment captured on film. A. J. Higgenson with his special Vauxhall designed to win him the record at Shelsley Walsh hill climb, about to go up the hill. From this car was born the 30/98 Vauxhall sports car. Higgenson's record of 55.2 seconds that day stood for fifteen years.

GENERAL MOTORS OVERSEAS OPERATIONS

Near the end of the 30/98's reign an interesting change was made in the popular "Velox" four seater sports-tourer body style. At the time, an international fad dictated building car bodies with a nautical flavor, the so-called "boat-tail" body for sporty cars. The style was perhaps best applied to some beautiful little Bugattis of the middle twenties, but it was also used on everything from a pert $1000 Essex to several $20,000 Duesenbergs. At Vauxhall, one of the works drivers, A. J. Hancock, became fond of the boat-tail styling and persuaded the factory to build a special edition of the OE 30/98 as a very sporty, topless, boat-tail roadster. The result was a handsome, stylish, V-windshield car called the "Wensum." The saucy little Wensum was a more attractive car than the old Velox, yet it failed to catch on and only seventeen were built.

In 1925 England was in the midst of a recession and retrenchment was the word with motorcar executives. Vauxhall Motors, Ltd. was one of the casualties. It was sold that year to General Motors. Big business's interest in something with such limited mass market appeal as a sports car, even a successful one, was small, and the OE 30/98 was dropped quietly in 1926. A few more were made up from spare parts and the last one left Luton early in 1928, an undramatic end for a dramatic car. Still, individualistic Vauxhalls continued to be built for awhile. The Hurlingham sports version was built on the 20/60 R-type chassis, and the 20/60 R in its more usual form as a touring car was an aristocratic-looking vehicle favored by the Prince of Wales (now Duke of Windsor). But the die was cast. In 1930 the GM-Vauxhall combine launched a "new emphasis" with a low priced sedan called the "Cadet" and by the middle thirties Vauxhall pretty well meant a middle-sized, inexpensive sedan—an English Chevrolet.

One of the great sports cars of the Golden Age, the 30/98 Vauxhall, in its most familiar form as the "Velox" sports/tourer. Between 1920–23 the 30/98 scored 75 first places in competition.

GENERAL MOTORS OVERSEAS OPERATIONS

The 30/98 powerplant; prosaic but potent. The engine was no forecast of the future, but it has passed the years gracefully. In 1953 a 25-year-old 30/98 lapped a French track at 107 mph average and took the straights at 120 mph.

GENERAL MOTORS OVERSEAS OPERATIONS

Discontinuance did little to dim British enthusiasm for the pre-GM Vauxhall. In fact, it seemed to intensify it. The factory had not officially competed since 1923 but that did not prevent private owners from racing. One of them, named R. J. Munday, entered his OE 30/98 in the Gold Star Race of 1932 at Weybridge and amazed almost everyone, except other Vauxhall fans, by lapping the track at 114.32 mph. Like Colt's single-action .45 revolver and Bowie's blade, sporting Vauxhalls seem to have a casual indifference to time and era. The very healthy ghosts of Laurence Pomeroy's cars still survive, and often not as pampered "antique cars" but as what they are—sports cars. At Oulton Park in Cheshire, England where the Vintage Sports Car Club has its two-and-a-half-mile track, it is not unusual to see a forty-five-year-old Vauxhall doing what it was built to do—being driven fast. And it is not just weekend fun and froth. Everyone is as serious as if it were the latest Ferrari at Le Mans, except that they seem to smile a little more often.

For the skeptics, Vauxhall addicts have a favorite story. In 1953, a 30/98 owner ferried his car across the Channel to the Montlhery track in France to see what it could do. This detour was necessary because the legendary old Brooklands

The sporty doorless and topless "Wensum" version of the 30/98.
GENERAL MOTORS OVERSEAS OPERATIONS

track, an RAF base during the war, had fallen victim to a housing development. The gentleman's name was T. H. Plowman, and the French stewards were a bit wary of having him drive his quarter-century-old machine flat out. When the run was over apology was in order. As Plowman warmed up the tall, homely car it began to hit its stride. Running very nicely it lapped the track at a 107 mph average (best lap 108.7) and devoured the straightaway at a cool 120 mph! Not at all bad for a twenty-five-year-old car with an obsolete engine and all the aerodynamic qualities of King Farouk.

Laurence Pomeroy's son, a famous automotive writer and

Laurence Pomeroy's son, the famous automotive writer, at speed in his father's greatest triumph, a Prince Henry Vauxhall, vintage 1914.

GENERAL MOTORS OVERSEAS OPERATIONS

pungent commentator on the mobile scene, still drives what some regard as his father's greatest triumph, a Prince Henry Vauxhall, vintage 1914. A few years ago he brought it to America to compete in the Anglo-American Vintage Rally, which among other calisthenics included a short trip across Times Square at the brisk clip of fifty miles an hour. Pomeroy the Younger, who uses his Prince Henry somewhat like an American suburbanite might rely on his trusty VW, enjoys pointing to its merits after more than a half century of use. It will still hit its World War I prime of 75 mph (which, he casually throws out, is almost universally the legal limit in America) and cruise comfortably at 60. In accordance with the original manual, it will still pass the suggested test for the clutch: "If the clutch is working well . . . a top speed (gear) start along the level can be accomplished with ease." But he dotes on another endearing characteristic, the praiseworthy suitability of the Prince Henry for picnics, at which the running board can be used as "either seat or table." Not many sports cars can make that claim.

Chapter 5

ETTORE BUGATTI-HIS EARLY PERIOD

In the beautiful green panorama of the Loire valley stands a picturesque old chateau, rising from a gentle hilltop like the vision of an ancient romantic fairy tale. Inside, the visitor is dazzled by a virtual avalanche of elegance; statuary, tapestry hung walls, rococo plaster ceilings, old masters as commonplace as Coke bottles. Presently, the guest is guided to the master's drawing room: very tasteful, very proper, very French. But here the more ordinary symbols of culture fade into the background as all eyes focus on an unexpected and unusual *objet d'art*—a vintage Bugatti sports car.

"It was," explains the owner, "the only humane and proper thing to do when I retired the car." So, a wall of the chateau was broken through, the Bugatti rolled in onto a Persian carpet, and the wall reconstructed. To the small but fiercely passionate number of *Bugattistes*, enshrining one of *le Patron's* creations in a drawing room is an unusual but hardly extreme measure of devotion. And it is not the only time that a Bugatti has been displayed as art rather than as engineering, a view shared by the Metropolitan Museum of Art. Bugatti is unquestionably the most coveted car in history, and possession of one is more of a religious cult than simple ownership. When Paris was occupied during World War II, a Type 41 was regarded as a national treasure, much the same as the Louvre's Rembrandts and Rubens, and French patriots secreted one in a sewer, resting on blocks, so that the Nazis would not carry it off as spoils of war. Reportedly, a young Parisian mademoiselle of the 1930s named Violet Nozier "did in" a rich uncle so that her inheritance would buy her boyfriend a Bugatti, although another version of the story has her as a restless wife who poisoned her husband, collected his insurance, and drove off into the sunset with a new Bugatti and friend. Maybe it is two separate stories—or a continuation of the same one. Normally, Bugattis excite somewhat less violent passion and more enduring devotion, and in some families Bugattis have been handed down like heirloom silver to be savored and held in trust for unborn sons.

It is not easy to explain the enigma of Ettore Bugatti and his cars. The Golden Age was well populated with men talented in the technology that makes cars go, both well and fast. There were unyielding perfectionists like Sir Henry Royce, brilliant innovators like Dr. Ferdinand Porsche, and imaginative creators like Harry C. Stutz. But there was no one quite like Ettore Bugatti. No one who lived like a feudal lord on a great factory-estate, no one whose thinking was so astonishingly self-contained, and no one who was so like a character out of a Jules Verne novel. He has justly been called an artist, and undoubtedly that is the description that suited, and pleased, him most. For if Henry Ford was a businessman whose medium was the automobile, then Bugatti was an artist in the same medium who never produced anything less than museum quality.

Ettore Bugatti was born in Milan in 1881, and as a teenager he was no more comprehensible to his art-loving parents than the young people of today are to theirs. Papa Carlo Bugatti was a painter, sculptor and engraver, and Ettore's older brother Rembrandt showed promise as a sculptor too and became famous for his animal studies. So it was naturally expected that Ettore would follow his art education at the Brera Academy by attending the Milan School of Fine Arts and further distinguish the respected reputation of the family Bugatti. But, instead, the bright and sensitive boy was enflamed in a passionate romance, not with one of the bouncy, black-eyed young signorinas of Milano, but with the equally fickle young automobile. When he was sixteen Bugatti got a part-time job at the bicycle shop of Prinetti & Stucchi, bought one of their bikes, and rebuilt it to suit himself. He installed a 1.25 hp De Dion-Bouton gas engine. In 1899 he entered his three-wheeler in seven races, won three, and took second and third places in two more. A four-wheel car—with a motor for each wheel—was unsuccessful. But Bugatti's non-conformity had, in the ancient tradition of the arts, attracted a patron. The Count Gulinelli de Ferrara was sufficiently impressed by the lively young man, his piles of drawings, and enthusiastic confidence to back his new project. The Count's faith was not misplaced and Ettore responded with a brilliantly advanced car. The four-cylinder, overhead-valve engine had a bore and stroke of 90 x 120 mm. The car had a four speed gearbox, chain drive, and contact battery ignition. It must have been a massive and intimidating undertaking for a boy of Ettore's short experience, but he plunged into the project with the same confidence that carried him throughout his career. He made the mechanical drawings, directed the foundry work, polished the metal, and assembled the parts himself. The car ran well and reached 40 mph, and Ettore immediately began calculating ways to increase the speed.

The next year, 1901, the nineteen-year-old's new car was exhibited at the Milan International Exposition. Ettore was never known for reticence, and the enthusiastic reception the car received gave a great boost to his natural Italian effervescence. A Milanese sporting journal effused over his genius and part of their praise was especially prophetic of the light, high-performance car he would pioneer and perfect to the state of an art. *La Gazetta dello Sport* said of the builder of the "Bugatti-Gulinelli carriage": "The engaging dare-devil of

Italian motorcycling conceived the idea of producing a kind of light vehicle which was not at the time on the market. It would not be the minute and very fragile vehicle too similar to the bicycle nor yet the complicated, useless, and costly mastodon, and this first attempt made a very good job of it, a triumph in fact; a small carriage, simple and most potent with a twelve horsepower four cylinder motor, capable of exacting daily service and of very great speed if necessary."

Baron De Dietrich, a steel magnate who had just ventured into the promising new world of automobiles, saw the Bugatti exhibit at Milan and was impressed. In fact, he was impressed enough to pay the equivalent of about $10,000 to hire this Italian boy to design cars for him. In the Bugatti family the De Dietrich offer precipitated a moment of truth. Ettore was a minor and could enter into no such contract unless Papa Carlo signed for him, and the elder Bugatti knew that, once such success came to his son from cars, a traditional career in

An early Bugatti drawing glances at an Italian vintage car meeting. Car in the foreground is a 1910 Benz.

art would be lost. But Papa Carlo signed, and unknowingly gave the Bugatti family its best known artist.

The association with De Dietrich would be one of several for Bugatti over the next decade, and the immediate result was a 24-hp, four-cylinder car of 114 x 130 mm bore and stroke which performed like a much larger machine. Ettore later designed for Emile Mathis at Strasbourg in German Alsace-Lorraine, worked independently for a time, and then became manager of the Deutz Works at Cologne, which kindly provided its young executive with a small villa. It was this villa, or rather its wine cellar, which would go down in history as the birthplace of the first *pur sang*, or thoroughbred, Bugatti. While he was designing a small 3.2-litre car for Deutz by day, Bugatti was working on an even smaller 1.3-litre machine in the wine cellar at night.

Ettore had great faith in the little car, and his enthusiasm was contagious. This time the "angel" was the father of Pierre de Vizcaya, a rising young race driver, who conveniently happened to be an official of the Bank of Darmstadt and to like automobiles. He showed Ettore an abandoned dyeing works at Molsheim, a quaint village in Alsace watched over by the brooding Vosges Mountains. Vizcaya arranged to finance the place and Bugatti and Ernest Friderich, his mechanic-driver-friend from his Strasbourg days with Mathis, moved in and set up shop in January 1910. It was a modest beginning. The building where the first Bugattis were built was a timber and plaster affair hardly bigger than a two-car garage in suburbia, and Friderich was left to whitewash its walls while Bugatti went off to buy machine tools.

The cars Ettore Bugatti began to build at Molsheim were truly unique; the world had never seen anything like them before. He sold only five of them that first year, but those five did more to establish his genius than five hundred ordinary cars could have done. The original *pur sang*, or Type 13, was properly a *voiturette*, a small, light car. Its specifications were almost comic in a day of multi-litered monsters. It had a wheelbase of a scant 78 inches and weighed only

The oldest surviving Bugatti, a Type 13 built at Molsheim, probably in 1910. With this basic design, Bugatti established his early reputation as an independent maker of small and remarkably quick sports cars, often recording amazing success against much larger cars.

COURTESY J. KUBA, DIRECTOR, NATIONAL TECHNICAL MUSEUM, PRAGUE

660 pounds. A Type 13 which ran at the Gaillon Hill Climb fully equipped, fueled, and with driver and passenger aboard weighed in at only 1168 pounds. The secret of the Type 13's sparkle lay in its tiny, toy-like, four-cylinder, 65 x 100-mm, 1.3-litre engine with overhead camshaft and two valves per cylinder. It was the last word in engine efficiency, running up to 3000 rpm and giving some 60 mph, in itself a minor miracle for such a small car in 1910. A French automotive writer who drove a Type 13 for the first time was astonished by the car, and called it "That Lilliputian box of speed."

Even in this very first car to carry the famous red and white Bugatti oval we can observe Ettore's fierce passion for underhood artistry. Everywhere there is a delicate sense of propriety and balance, from the four merging arms of the manifold to the hand polished bronze cam covers which carried the bold script signature "Ettore Bugatti." Already it seemed more like sculpture than mere machinery.

The Type 13 Bugatti was more than just a small, fast car. It was a high performance sports machine built with the meticulous precision of a fine watch and then perfectly miniaturized without the slightest loss of performance. It was actually hard to believe: a tiny car that had the speed of one nearly ten times its engine size, the roadability of a car several times its weight, a steering precision that was uncannily alive and accurate, a four-speed gearbox of amazing pleasantness and petiteness (one test driver reported that the gate could be slipped into his vest pocket)—a car that could deliver forty miles to the imperial gallon.

One of the first people to drive the Type 13 and to tell about it was an Englishman named W. F. Bradley, who would come to know Bugatti well through the years. His 1910 road test of the Type 13 was well laced with superlatives and he told of chasing a big-engined Benz "Prince Henry sports car through the Paris suburbs and being able "to keep within fifty yards of his pointed stern all the way, and with less discomfort than is experienced in many cars three times the size and weight." As for the practical side of the Type 13 Bugatti, Bradley was even more benign: "In city traffic the little car proved as remarkable as on the straightaway stretches for, being small, it could worm through where larger cars were held up. It was wonderfully quick in acceleration, absolutely silent on low gears, while the changes were made without a click being heard. As a runabout, where one or more large cars are kept, the little Bugatti seems ideal, for on the open roads it is as fast as any of the larger mounts, and in traffic it is quicker because of its handiness. Its upkeep is a mere trifle."

In order to spread Mr. Bradley's sort of satisfaction some public proof of the Bugatti magic was in order. So a Type 13 with Friderich as driver was entered in the 1911 French Grand Prix, which was formula *libre* that year. The little Bugatti took second place, but the effect could hardly have been more jolting if it had won outright. It trounced every big car in the race except a monster 10.5-litre Fiat, which was also a technically advanced car with overhead cam and four valves per cylinder. The Type 13 also distinguished itself at the famous Gaillon Hill Climb in 1910 and 1911, but its most spectacular run came in 1912 when it was first in the touring class and second only to Fritz Erle's enormous 21.5-litre "Blitzen Benz." More victories against ridiculous odds followed, and mystified people began saying things like "Whence the power comes from only Monsieur Bugatti knows!"

In 1911 Bugatti built seventy-five cars, but it was perfection, not production, that interested him. He once wrote: "I could build six times the number of cars if I were satisfied to let anything with a Bugatti nameplate go forth onto the road as a Bugatti. But I am not. Our disposition, here, is that we will not allow to leave our gates any car which we are not satisfied will represent us with credit." And for all *le Patron's* flamboyance, it was not press agentry; he really meant it, and he kept on meaning it all through the pursuit of his art and craft. Almost immediately Ettore began improving his car and, in a certain sense, he never really finished until World War II put him out of business thirty years later. In the years between, he built scores of models, the world's most exclusive and expensive luxury car, and masterpieces of sports cars and Grand Prix machinery which all the world envied. But, despite obvious technical progress, the philosophical similarity between his cars of 1909 and of 1939 was striking and uncanny.

The earliest change Bugatti made in the little Type 13 was to lengthen the wheelbase, thus creating the Types 15 and 17 which appeared as a four seater sports tourer and a very quaint looking little touring car "*pour la ville et le tourisme.*" Perhaps this is as good a time as any to sound a warning not to take the Bugatti type numbers and nomenclature too literally. They have likely caused sleepless nights to automotive scholars and no one has yet fathomed them quite fully. The renowned Bugatti expert H. G. Conway points out that Bugatti used different type numbers to catalogue different chassis lengths of what were essentially the same car, especially in his early period, which creates a sort of havoc for the novice cutting his teeth on Bugatti. The important improvement on the original Thirteen came in 1914 when a 16-valve version was first built and gave considerably hotter performance. Ettore was now beginning to flourish—he built 175 cars in 1913—but the bullet that cut down Austrian Archduke Franz Ferdinand also cut short Bugatti's aspirations for the new 16-valve cars, the Type 22 and the Type 23. But it did not prevent him from sending a car to Indianapolis in 1914 and to the American Grand Prize at San Francisco in 1915. Neither was blessed with particularly good luck. The 1914 100 x 180 mm Indianapolis car held third place for about 85% of the

It was with his 16-valve Type 22 or "Brescia" that Bugatti really began to build his reputation as a master builder of sports cars just after World War I. In sporting trim the Brescia was good for 100 mph, or 70 mph as a tourer. Here, a 40-year-old Brescia corners at Prescott Hill Climb in England.

MONTAGU MOTOR MUSEUM
PHOTO: MICHAEL E. WARE

race until the ball bearings of the driving pinion gave way. In the 1915 Grand Prize, the Bugatti only made it to the sixth lap (out of 104), when the ignition failed.

When the war came, Friderich went back to France to join his artillery regiment (Molsheim was on German soil) and Ettore found himself with five of his 16-valve cars and the German army literally over the next hill. He carefully swabbed three of them in heavy grease and buried them, then took the other two home to Milan and later to Paris.

In wartime, Bugatti's talents for extracting unusual power and efficiency out of lightweight engines had obvious value in aircraft. Working at Puteaux on the outskirts of Paris, he designed two aeroengines: a straight eight and a double bank 16-cylinder engine, literally a "double eight." The bigger engine was an inspired and typically Bugatti piece of work, and it caught the eye of an American commission that had been sent to Europe to look for a good airplane engine which could be produced in America. Charles B. King was selected to father the big Bugatti here, and the Duesenberg brothers of Elizabeth, New Jersey, got the contract to build it. Bugatti's associate, Friderich (now a *Croix de Guerre* holder), was promptly yanked out of his regiment near Nancy and hustled off to New Jersey to help with *le Patron's* big engine.

Bugatti's 16-cylinder engine is a monument to pure Leonardo-like genius unadulterated by the dogma of a technical school. Bugatti had no formal engineering education, yet with one small defect the design he sent to America represented the most advanced and efficient aircraft engine in existence. Rated at from 500 to 520 hp, the big 48-valve engine gave over one horsepower for each two pounds of weight. And for good measure Ettore had designed a hollow propellor shaft to accommodate a 37-mm repeating cannon. The one oversight in the engine, although Ettore saw it otherwise, was the retention of an old-style splash oiling system, for which the Duesenberg-built models substituted a pressure lubricating system. This was a stubborn point with Bugatti. Even when the less positive splash or drip lubrication caused bearing

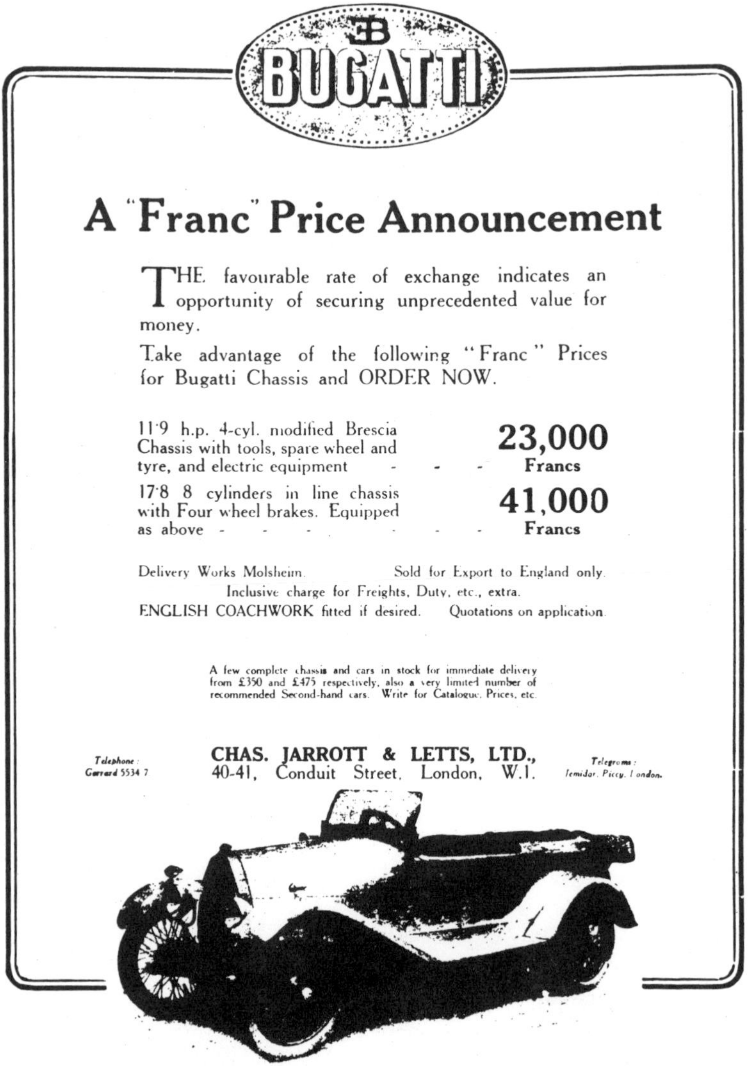

Advertisement for the Brescia Bugatti and the 8-cylinder Type 30 which was introduced late in 1922. The English representative, Charles Jarrott, was a noted early race driver, competing in the Paris-Madrid, 1903 Gordon Bennett, and other classic races.

trouble in his cars he went to the extreme of using roller bearing crankshafts to circumvent it until he finally accepted pressure lubrication in 1928. Like his later reluctance to supercharge his engines, it was another example of his hesitancy to rely on an idea which had not been born in the Bugatti brain.

Despite the design change in the lubricating system, Duesenberg's president, J. R. Harbeck, grew ecstatic over Ettore's engine in his report to the U.S. Government. He wrote: "The use of sixteen comparatively small cylinders results in a perfectly balanced running condition and perfect synchronization. The size of the cylinders permits operation with safety at high engine speeds, and the skilled adoption of the gear principle permits the use of these engine speeds at *useful* propellor speeds. . . . This represents the outstanding advantage of the Bugatti motor over any other motor approaching it in power. . . . The great power, compactness, flexibility, and reliability permits its use in a variety of planes . . . from the very high powered combat plane to the heaviest type of bombing and sea plane. . . . In conclusion, it may be stated that the Bugatti motor is to be regarded as a fully developed product subject to possible small refinements as production progresses, but at the present moment suitable for general use. It is a significant fact that in spite of the changes in design the third motor submitted to the fifty-four hour endurance test went through this test successfully. It may be noted that the motor as at present built is essentially a low compression engine, and that as need develops there is every reasonable expectation of securing very much greater power by an increase in compression." Only a few of the big Bugatti engines were actually built by Duesenberg, about forty in all, but they served Bugatti well as public relations pieces.

Except for a sports plane which he designed in the late thirties for the Coupe Deutsche (actually a thinly disguised fighter), Bugatti had no special interest in airplane engines other than doing his duty for his adopted France. The 16-cylinder engine would have been merely a sidelighted achievement of his career if it had not been exposed to the appreciative mind of the brothers Duesenberg. Fred Duesenberg was fascinated by the big motor, and the guns were hardly quiet on the western front when he began adapting it as the heart of a straight-eight racing motor. Rife with Bugatti-isms, the engine powered the only American car ever to win an important European race until Ford came to Le Mans a generation later, and it firmly established the "eight" as the great and lasting love of American drivers. Ettore, assisted by Fred Duesenberg, had unwittingly changed the whole course of automotive development on this side of the Atlantic. It should be mentioned, however, that Bugatti had been experimenting with the eight-cylinder concept since 1911, when he coupled a pair of Type 13s together "by means of a rubberized leather flywheel." Ernest Friderich drove the 2.8-litre car and said of it: "Proud and overcome with emotion was the happy driver. This car reached a speed of 86 mph, whereas the car used in the Grand Prix at Le Mans did not exceed 66 mph."

While Ettore Bugatti was extracting astonishing power and speed from his tiny 1.3-litre sports car, other Italians were at work at the opposite end of the scale. Here, the big displacement, 4-cylinder chain-drive concept at its most preposterous extreme; the 1910 FIAT "Mephistopheles" which produced 300 hp from 28.3 litres!

FIAT

The eight-cylinder engine would become very important to Bugatti, as it was to Duesenberg. His epic cars would be mainly eights (the Type 45 and the Type 47 would be 16-cylinder), and it is curious to note that he totally rejected the six-cylinder concept.

As we have seen, the war clipped off Bugatti's budding little 16-valve sports car before he had a chance to do anything with it. These were the cars Bugatti had buried at Molsheim: precise, petit machines that could turn over seventy in touring trim and could be tuned to even higher revolutions in order to break a hundred in open competition. The balanced and beautiful Bugatti "horseshoe" radiator had clearly begun to take shape on these cars, although it still resembled an egg slightly and the engine compartment vaguely suggested an elongated canned ham. In 1920 Ettore dispatched three of these cars south to Le Mans for the Voiturette Grand Prix, one each for Friderich, de Vizcaya and Baccoli. The red and white enamel Bugatti oval set the pace from the beginning. Pierre de Vizcaya's number 1 held the lead with only three laps to go when it pulled into the pits. When Ettore himself diagnosed the noises coming from the engine it was clear that his reluctance over pressure lubrication had so torpedoed the bearings that it was doubtful if the little car could cover even one more lap. Rather than suffer the embarrassment of having the car fail on the track itself, Bugatti walked to the front end and unscrewed the radiator cap. Under the rules, only de Vizcaya's riding mechanic, Mischall, could lay a finger on the car, and number 1 was summarily disqualified. But Friderich in number 23 was still going strong and managed to get home twenty minutes ahead of his nearest competitor.

A few lesser races were also won that year, but it was 1921 that might be called the real beginning of Bugatti's legendary invincibility. In September, four cars were sent to the Italian Voiturette Grand Prix at Brescia. The Italian rules allowed a slightly more generous engine displacement and the Bugattis were bored out to 1453 cubic centimeters (68 x 100 mm) and had two plugs per cylinder and dual carburetors. This time there was no holding any of them back, conservative lubrication or not. It was Bugatti, *un*, *deux*, *trois*, *quatre*.

Ettore capitalized on the spectacular across-the-board Italian victory by calling the model the "Brescia" and he sold not de-tuned models but exact duplicates of the Brescia cars to anyone who wanted to drive the best sports car that money could buy in 1921. Those who bought were eminently satisfied, and some of those cars are still pleasing owners today. An Englishman named Raymond Mays bought one of the early Brescia Bugattis and did wonders with it. Among other joys it is said to have given him 6700 rpm (even Ettore never claimed that!) after some brain surgery calibre tuning, and as a matter of record it gave him the fastest hill climb car in the country in the middle 1920s. The Brescia was typical of Bugatti's philosophy of the *pur sang* sports car that kidded no one, and at from $1800 to $2300 chassis price it was a thoroughbred car at an equally thoroughbred bargain. A longer wheelbase car (93 inches), a touring version of only slightly less liveliness, called the "Brescia Modifié," was also available at a mere $1600.

The Brescia was a big thing for Bugatti; the car increased his currency and prestige enormously. But it was just the beginning of what some people insist was the purest part of the Golden Age of sports cars.

Chapter 6

THE GREAT AMERICAN SPORTS CAR

"*You have to be nuts to drive a Stutz!*" was a favorite taunt among Mercer fans in those days before World War I when the lustiest two American sports cars were slugging it out like a pair of bareknuckle champions on every dirt track between Philadelphia and Santa Monica. Besides being a brilliant, innovating engineer, Harry C. Stutz had a Madison Avenue mind and a flair for flamboyant names and slogans. No one has ever traced it directly to him, but the chances are that Stutz just might have had a hand in the equally famous reprise: "*There's nothing worser than a Mercer!*"

Harry Stutz built his first car in 1897 when he was twenty-one. Or rather he converted somebody's buggy into a horseless carriage and inaugurated his fancy for exotic names by calling it "Old Hickory." For a poor farmer's son there was no expensive technical education to develop his natural talents, so Stutz forged his own education in the shops and factories around his native Ohio and later in the growing automobile center of Indianapolis. Stutz's early schooling in creating great cars was informal but hardly ineffective. His self-imposed apprenticeship with an assortment of car-component contractors gave him practical working experience with every part of a car from carburetors to tires. For a time he worked for the American Motor Car Company and began to put his bits and pieces of knowledge together by designing an engine and the advanced, road-rugging "American Underslung" chassis for them.

By 1910 Harry Stutz, trading as the "Stutz Auto Parts Company," was designing and building his own components for car makers, mainly rear axles and gearboxes. It occurred to him that the best way to test and sell his wares was to install them in a successful racing machine. Although he had a taste of track dust as both driver and mechanic, Stutz was never so wholly committed to racing for its own sake as were, say, the Duesenberg brothers or Ettore Bugatti. Stutz shrewdly saw racing for what it was at the time; a tool for selling cars. Astrologers would confidently point to Stutz's September-born quality of practical materialism backed by an "instinctive love for work."

That love for work and respect for proper preparation went into the original Stutz in full measure. The essence of Stutz skill shaped the chassis and drive train, although the Stutz-designed engine was built by the Wisconsin Motor Company. Stutz was serious when he said that he wanted to see what his newly designed machine would do. Few men would have had the confidence, or nerve, to enter an untested and brand new car—actually the very first Stutz ever built—in a brand new race called the Indianapolis "500." A Marmon driven by Raymond Harroun won that first "500" in May 1911 at an average of 74.9 mph, but it was the new Stutz back in eleventh place, just out of the prize money, that would really earn the gravy. Running steadily at an average of 68 mph, the maiden Stutz didn't even strain a bolt while carefully groomed all-out racing machinery was falling by the wayside right and left. The smaller engine could not give the speed of the bigger racers, but the absolute reliability of the new car gave sloganeer Harry Stutz "The Car That Made Good in A Day."

Stutz Bearcat—a magic name, a great American sports car, and a visual, visceral experience.

THE MUSEUM OF AUTOMOBILES

Stutz had not really conceived his car as a pure racer but rather as a solid and reliable car for conventional customers. In a rare example of consumer perspicacity, his potential audience sensed Stutz's skill and integrity and deluged him with more orders than he could fill. The Stutz was launched and off to a flying start. Right after finishing up the racing season with a second place in the Fairmount Park Road Race in Philadelphia and a third place in the Santa Monica Road Race, Harry Stutz got down to the business of building automobiles for sale. And extraordinary cars they were, these first-born Series A Stutzes. The chassis was a duplicate of that of the durable Indianapolis car, with a 390-cubic-inch, T-head engine that could turn out 60 horsepower at 1500 rpm. Stutz's specialized experience was evident in the rear axle which carried the transmission built integrally with the differential. These special rear axle units were built by his original company, Stutz Auto Parts Company, which he merged with his car production company, the Ideal Motor Car Company, in 1913 to form the Stutz Motor Car Company. In the same year, Stutz started building his own engines and consolidated his capacity to produce five hundred automobiles a year.

Public acceptance of the new cars soared with Stutz track successes: a fourth place with a 64.2 mph average in the eighth Vanderbilt Cup Race in 1912, another fourth in that race in 1914, a second place in the tenth Vanderbilt Cup run in San Francisco in 1915, and another second in the final run for the Vanderbilt Cup at Santa Monica in 1916, third place in the American Grand Prize at Savannah in 1912, and second places in 1915 and 1916. In 1913 nearly 100,000 people at $2.00 a head showed up at Indianapolis to see a French

Stutz's pre-World War I 16-valve four-cylinder racing engine, proprietary built by Wisconsin Motor Manufacturing Co.

SMITHSONIAN INSTITUTION

Peugeot win and Spencer Wishart and Charles Merz battle it out with a Mercer and a Stutz for second and third. The next year a Stutz with Barney Oldfield up was fifth and the only American car to finish near the right end of the pack. By the middle of 1913, Stutz had run in nearly a hundred races and captured twenty-nine firsts, three seconds, and five thirds. Some of the record entries speak best for themselves: at the Bakersfield Road Race, February 1912, "Finished over an hour ahead of nearest competitor"; at the Grand Prize, Milwaukee, October 1912, "The only American made car to finish the race and the smallest American made car that ever won 'place' in a Grand Prix race"; at Fresno, California, February 1913, "Mile track record for two hundred miles."

Stutz advertising played up the success at speed to the fullest. "Racing a car is concentrating its use."; "It is subjecting the car to every possible disadvantage in the shortest possible space of time. Out of that test comes either a car or a memory. Out of all the racing tests has come a better and truer Stutz." And what the ads didn't say was that the best was yet to come.

For 1914 Harry Stutz brought out a new line of cars called the Series E. His catalogue carried the headline "The Sturdy Stutz," and he laid a heavy hand on the robust, indestructible qualities of his cars. "You buy a Stutz like you buy a house or build a barn.", the catalogue counseled, "Foundations are put into the ground to stay and stick. Houses are regarded as real estate . . . a Stutz car is real estate." Harry Stutz knew that 1914 vintage Americans expected, and usually got, honest measure in whatever they bought; few makers of anything could sell shimmering "images" in those days and expect to survive. Buyers got what they paid for when they plunked down from $2000 to $2400 for a Series E Stutz, but in one particular model they got something more than they bargained for—a legend in the making. Stutz still indulged his fondness for names—he called his racing team "the Stutz White Squadron"—and he named the open sports version of his Series E cars the "Bearcat." Modestly, he described it as an automo-

bile "designed to meet the requirements of the customer desiring a car built along the general lines of a racing car, and with a slightly higher gear ratio than our regular torpedo roadster." Destined to bring immortality to the Stutz name, the Bearcat became the most famous American sports car in history. The last car to be called Bearcat was built in 1934, yet the name lives on with the same sort of endurance Harry Stutz built into all his cars.

The Bearcat was one of those rare creations that was more than the sum of its parts. Technically, the Bearcat was up to date, but it was hardly revolutionary. Stutz's experience with chassis and axle construction accounted for the straight-line drive, which used a double knuckle universal joint behind the clutch, torsion tube to the rear axle, and of course the three speed gearbox integral with the rear axle. The 4½-inch channel-steel frame rose two and a half inches at the rear to accommodate the straight-line drive. The front axle was a contract part supplied by Timken, with Timken roller bearings at the steering knuckles. The engine was an ordinary T-head design, available as either a 4¾ x 5½-inch, four-cylinder (390 cubic inches) or a 4 x 5-inch six (377 cubic inches), and it offered about sixty horsepower at 1500 rpm. By European standards of items like Ernest Henri's double-overhead-cam Peugeot racers, or the 1914 single-overhead-cam Mercedes GP cars, or even the new little Bugattis, it was a quite conventional power source. Yet the Stutz engine could make the Bearcat go at an honest 80 mph, which was more than most American roads could handle at the time, and it was an uncomplicated, trouble-free, and wonderfully durable piece of machinery.

But the Bearcat was not just a collection of mechanical parts, however well made and assembled. It was a visual, even visceral, experience. By racing car style standards of 1914, the

By 1920 the gauntness of the pre-war Bearcats had been filled in with sheet metal, and the car lost a lot of its timeless, elemental elegance in the modernization.

THE MUSEUM OF AUTOMOBILES

Bearcat's appearance was already dated, even old fashioned. Its profile looked much like that of the "Sixty" Mercedes of 1903 or those of the Locomobile racers of the early Vanderbilt classics. Yet, like those cars, the Bearcat reduced the performance car to its barest essentials. Harry Stutz saw the sports car as an elemental thing; a machine devoted to the business of moving fast. There were no frivolities such as doors, sides, windshield or a top, and no concessions to windcheating. The gaunt Bearcat was pure function. In 1914 the self-educated Stutz had sensed what designers and artists would struggle to say to the world over the next half century: that when form follows function the result can be pleasing—and enduring.

The rest of the Stutz line included a four- or six-cylinder touring car and a sedate high-roofed coupe that was supplied with "dark blue leather upholstery with tufted cushions of Turkish design, twelve inches thick, and with black walnut and broadcloth trimming." And there was one other model,

Although less with appeal than its heroic ancestor, the 1920 Stutz Bearcat was the prohibition era college boy's dream.
AUTOMOBILE MANUFACTURERS ASSOC.

Steering by Stutz.

AUTHOR'S PHOTO

a somewhat more "civilized" sports roadster, which lent proof to the proposition that the Bearcat was more than the sum of its parts. Catalogued as the "Torpedo Roadster," this car shared an identical chassis with the Bearcat, the same choice of engines and the same price tag. It was a most attractive little sports car, fitted with such niceties as doors and folding windscreen, and as a whole, rather more contemporary and comfortable than the austere Bearcat. Of the two cars, though, almost no one except for ardent Stutz fanciers remembers the roadster, while the sensual essentiality of the Bearcat will never be forgotten.

The introduction of the Bearcat also brought the great Stutz vs Mercer duel down to a personal participation level. Mercer already had its counterpart "Raceabout" on the market, and now owners of the great rivals could hurl challenges and those rhyming epithets at each other and pretend to be Barney Oldfield or Spencer Wishart as they settled scores on dusty back roads. Each with its strong points, the two cars were perfectly suited for such informal match races and they guaranteed to keep the feud going.

The Stutz was the right thing at the right time and place,

A Stutz four-passenger "Sport Model K" of the early Twenties out for a spin.

AUTOMOBILE MANUFACTURERS ASSOC.

and the company prospered. Most people agreed that Harry Stutz gave them a square deal, but inevitably there was a finicky customer. As the story goes, one day he showed up at a Stutz dealer in New York claiming that the engine in his touring car was no good. The Stutz customer got his money back, and Harry Stutz was asking himself, "How can I turn this to my advantage?" The answer was to take the suspect engine (which Stutz mechanics found perfectly normal), mount it in a Bearcat chassis, ship it to California, and have a motorcycle race driver named Cannonball Baker drive it back across country as hard and fast as he could go.

Tommy Milton poses with the pristine white winner of the 1923 Indianapolis "500," which was really a Miller racer carrying the H.C.S. initials.

INDIANAPOLIS MOTOR SPEEDWAY CORP.

The voyage of Baker's Bearcat remains something of a minor odyssey in the history of the motorcar, perhaps even the American equivalent of the run of the Silver Ghost in the 1907 Scottish Reliability Trials. Basically, the car was stock, except for a double set of Hartford shocks at the rear, the absence of fenders and running boards, and a slightly enlarged clearance between pistons and cylinder walls. Extra equipment was limited to an additional spare tire, an extra gallon of oil under the hood in a tin can, a 2½-gallon water bag hanging from each side lamp, an axe, and a .44-calibre Colt six-shooter strapped to the steering column. Baker blasted off from the offices of the *San Diego Union* on May 6, 1915, with William Sturm on board, a reporter from the *Indianapolis News* who provided no help beyond taking notes and pictures. On the first day, Baker covered 409 miles in fifteen hours and added 592 miles the next day. The road took him over the Arizona desert, New Mexican mountains and rivers, Texas prairie, Oklahoma mud, and everything else a rugged continent could throw at him and the Bearcat. Exactly eleven days, seven hours and fifteen minutes later, a very muddy Bearcat pulled up at 42nd Street and Broadway with the "no good" engine "purring like an overgrown housecat," in Sturm's words. The transcontinental run was documented thoroughly by Sturm, who wrote "As for the car, it was not the tires, it was not the engine, it was not the assembly that made the trip possible. It was the car in the aggregate, it was the car as a whole." No one, however, recorded any comments from the former owner of the "no good" engine.

While the Bearcat era was in full swing Harry Stutz was busy concerning himself with high performance racing engines. Turning to European inspiration, he broke completely with the old T-head engine and entered the 1915 racing season with a startling new design. With overhead camshaft and

Harry Stutz flanked by a pair of enigmatic "H.C.S. Specials." The irony was that Stutz won the "500" with a non-Stutz car.
INDIANAPOLIS MOTOR SPEEDWAY CORP.

Stripped chassis of the H.C.S. Special.

INDIANAPOLIS MOTOR SPEEDWAY CORP.

four valves per cylinder, the new engine was a four-cylinder of 3.8 x 6.5-inch bore and stroke and 296-cubic-inch displacement to bring it just under the 300 CI limit for Indianapolis. The car was certainly one of the most advanced in America, and after a flurry of success in California racing early in 1915, three Stutz specials were readied for Indianapolis. These, of course, were the years just before World War I when international racing was dominated by the Henri-designed DOHC Peugeots and the SOHC 1914 Mercedes GP cars; such was the competition the fresh Stutzes faced at the 1915 "500." Although the Stutz team could not overcome the slashing thrust of Ralph De Palma's Mercedes and Dario Resta's Peugeot, they put up a fine fight and captured third, fourth and seventh places. Stutz finished out the '15 season in glory, and recorded the high-water mark of his presence on the bricks, boards, and dirt. Racing had served its purpose and Stutz had other things to think about: expanding production, a war, and an invasion of the Stutz Motor Car Company by Wall Street.

In refinancing his company to keep it expanding Harry Stutz went public, and promptly ran into one situation that his makeshift automotive education hadn't covered—the upper echelons of high finance. Within a short time after Stutz shares began trading on Wall Street, the Stutz Motor Car Company was in outside hands, and for the first time in over ten years Harry Stutz had a boss. This couldn't—and didn't—last very long, and in 1919 Stutz was out and in the same position the Brothers Maserati were to find themselves a generation later—operating a very small company and competing against a much larger one bearing his own name.

The new product was christened the "H.C.S." after Stutz's initials. The unimaginative acronym didn't sound much like Stutz and neither did the car itself. The first edition appeared in December 1920, and the reception was about as warm as the weather. Quality was high, but coming from the man who built the Bearcat and homeric racing machines, the H.C.S. seemed dull and undistinguished. But there was one flash of fortune: the 1923 winner at Indianapolis was astonishingly the "H.C.S. Special," which covered the distance in 5½ hours at an average speed of 91 mph. It would have been even more astonishing had the Indy car been the H.C.S. itself instead of the full-bred racing machine Stutz had bought from Miller. Despite the H.C.S. initials heading the winners list, the publicity did little to sell cars and Stutz's effort collapsed of its own weight in 1924, a sad epilogue to a grand career.

Meanwhile, dark machinations were going on with the shares of the Stutz Motor Car Company, in which enormous sums of money were made and lost. Ultimately, the company came under the control of Andrew Carnegie's protégé, steel magnate Charles M. Schwab. Obviously, a great deal was happening in the auto industry since Harry Stutz left the company bearing his name, yet the company was still relying on his designs with only slight variation. The first move to change this under Schwab's reign was the "Speedway Six." This was a car somewhat in the Stutz sporting tradition, but hardly avante garde: an overhead-valve, pushrod, six-cylinder of some

"JONES' STUTZ SPECIAL"
27
Firestone Balloon
L. CORUM, Driver – Milton Jones, Mech., and Relief Driver.
Indianapolis Motor Speedway 1930.
10TH PLACE WINNER
28322
KIRKPATRICK
619 W. WASH. S
INDPLS.

4.25 litres that offered about 80 hp. It represented a step forward out of the corporate confusion, but the Speedway Six set no records on either track or sales chart.

Harry Stutz was a self-made engineer who was weak in big business administration (although he died a wealthy man), Schwab was a tycoon who knew little about automobiles. What the Stutz Motor Car Company needed was a man who could master both fields—the world of the drawing office and machine shop and the world of the board room and business office. There was such a man. His name was Fred Moskovics, and Schwab—in his greatest contribution to the company—put him in control.

Moskovics was a well-educated engineer and apparently an intuitive businessman and administrator. He was not the classic creator who dreamed up ideas on which other men got rich. His career developed in the pioneer era of the motorcar before World War I, and he had been exposed to a multitude of ideas. With a few of his own thrown in for good measure, his dream was to synthesize the best of them and to create an ultimate machine. Stutz and Schwab gave him the chance.

Moskovics came to Stutz early in 1925 already armed with the basics of his dream car. The company spent a million dollars perfecting his plans and took the 1926 New York auto show by storm with the Series AA "Vertical Eight" Stutz. Like the European sports car builders, Moskovics laid heavy emphasis on a sophisticated chassis. For safety and road security at speed it had to be daringly low and very rigid. To accomplish this, Moskovics used a straight-line drive from the transmission to the rear (similar to that of the original Stutz) but added an underslung worm-geared rear axle assembly, a complex and expensive piece of metalwork that made the Stutz chassis fully five inches lower than that of its rivals.

In 1930 a nearly stock Stutz was entered in the Indianapolis "500" by Milton Jones and driven by Stutz driver L. L. Corum, finishing tenth.

INDIANAPOLIS MOTOR SPEEDWAY CORP.

The *ne plus ultra* of Stutz automobiles, the Super Bearcat DV-32; very possibly the finest sports car ever built in America.

THE MUSEUM OF AUTOMOBILES

The double dropped-frame rails were tied together with seven cross members to give the new Stutz an extraordinarily rigid chassis. The overall result was a lower, better handling and genuinely safer car than any of the Stutz contemporaries.

The advanced chassis was complemented by an equally advanced 4.7-litre, straight-eight engine that used an overhead camshaft to operate the two valves per cylinder. It was a particularly advanced engine on the American scene, sharing its sophistication only with the Duesenberg straight-eight. Interestingly, Stutz and Duesenberg shared several points of rapport: they both sought efficiency and speed through the best engineering of the day with little regard to cost; they both came early to the straight-eight concept; they both had connections with the genius of Ettore Bugatti and adapted it to their own advantage; and they were the only two American marques of the era to bring any sort of glory to U.S. cars at speed on foreign soil.

Moskovics' engine had been produced in cooperation with Stutz's chief engineer, Charles Greuter, whose familiarity with the overhead-cam engine went all the way back to the turn of the century. The design included dual ignition, high-pressure lubrication, and alloy connecting rods and pistons in line with the best engineering practices. But its high point of innovation lay in the wonderfully quiet chain drive that operated the overhead camshaft. At the small displacement of 289 cubic inches, the Stutz put out as much or more horsepower than expensive American cars of larger displacement, and it did it without being leaned upon at all. Still—there was room for considerable future development.

Traditionally, the name Stutz was almost a synonym for sports and speed, and the Series AA was a logical extension of that tradition. The Vertical Eight was in fact a pretty good forecast of what Harry Stutz might have built in 1926 had he

A Stutz Bearcat is probably the single most wanted automobile of all American cars, and the few surviving specimens are priced accordingly. So, enthusiasts have been known to improvise, such as with this re-built "roadster" on an old fire engine chassis.

AUTHOR'S PHOTO

kept control of the company. But big business was at the helm now and it steered a safe course toward the biggest profits—the carriage trade for luxury cars. An extensive advertising campaign was launched, with "Safety Stutz" as its key theme. The inbred excitement of the Stutz name was soft-pedaled and the new car was almost pictured as the ideal machine for milady to tool down to her dressmakers in. Ads emphasized such features as the rigid frame, safety glass, hefty bumpers (which would be welcomed back on today's cars), and an interesting touch called the "No Back" which permitted starting on hills without the slightest backward drift. The luxury angle was intensified in 1928 with an elegant line of custom bodies from Le Baron which clothed the Stutz chassis with the cream of the coachbuilder's art.

Despite the emphasis on the purely practical side of the Series AA, the sporty Stutz character shone through the safety-slanted ads in the posh magazines of the 1920s. Here and there could be found lines about the rakish low-slung lines, responsive acceleration (0–50 mph in fifteen seconds in top gear) and the snappy four-wheel hydraulic brakes. To some extent the new Stutz could be masqueraded as a luxury car but there was no denying that it was a sports car at heart. With somewhat suppressed glee the company began to acknowledge this fact as early as 1927 with the appearance of the Black Hawk Speedster and the serious return of Stutz to competition.

The first big expedition back to the track was the Stutz bid for the Stevens Challenge Trophy in 1927. The Challenge was started by Samuel B. Stevens of early racing fame and consisted of a twenty-four-hour endurance run for stock cars that ran for record only and not in direct competition. In essence it was a sort of Le Mans without the glamour and glory but with the grind of twenty-four hours at nearly full throttle. If there was one U.S. car in 1927 that was suitable for this sort of thing it was Stutz. Three Stutz cars were entered for the Challenge: a standard sedan, a lightweight Weymann fabric-bodied sedan (Moskovics' personal car) and the new Black Hawk Speedster. Even in late April the Indianapolis climate was still mean and the Stutz triumvirate ran through a St. Patrick's day-like combination of rain, snow and sleet. But a full day later the three cars were still running strong. The standard passenger version averaged 68.4 mph, the lightweight Weymann slightly less at 67.1 mph, and the stripped-down Black Hawk Speedster the best at 71.3 mph. It was a clear-cut victory, and the Trophy was Stutz property until a 490-cubic-inch Marmon V-16 took it away in 1931 with 78.9 mph.

Stutz gamely entered every competition it could and collected victories from Atlantic City to Pikes Peak. Throughout this period, Stutz demonstrated amazing dependability; ironically, the celebrated $25,000 Stutz vs Hispano-Suiza duel at Indianapolis was the single race in which a Stutz failed to finish because of mechanical failure, and even then the failure could be traced to an over-anxious driver who went against the planned strategy. A different and even more costly blow came shortly after the famous match race. Stutz's ace driver, Frank Lockhart, wanted a try at the land speed record and Stutz engineering and Miller engine expertise were married to create a car that would remain stable under the thrust of the more than 500 horsepower of the special V-16 three-litre engine. The Miller was installed in a Black Hawk chassis at the Stutz plant and covered with a narrow torpedo body with outrigger fenders. It was a handsome car, sleek and confident as it bristled over the sands of Daytona. Neatly lettered on Frank Lockhart's cockpit were the words "Stutz Black Hawk Special, Made in Indianapolis." The car fulfilled expectations as it went down the beach at 198 mph, but then at a still higher speed a tire blew out. The car crashed and Lockhart was killed.

The incident chilled Stutz's competition program but the development of sporting production cars, now well under way with the Black Hawk Speedster and the new Series BB cars for 1928, rolled on. The "expandable" Stutz engine was given ten more cubic inches and about twenty more horsepower in standard form. In all, the engine could now be had in four stages of development, with increasing compression ratios of up to 6.25:1 and with eight axle ratios. Despite all the lush coachbuilder's exercises from Le Baron and Fleetwood laid out in the catalogues, it grew harder to camouflage the Stutz as another Packard, Pierce-Arrow, or Lincoln. Any hope of concealing the Stutz as anything less than the red-blooded sports machine that it was finally vanished in 1928 when a privately owned Series BB Stutz was entered in the Le Mans race. In the twenties, of course, Le Mans seemed almost the exclusive preserve of the great green Bentleys, and a contest between W.O. Bentley's battle wagons and the one car that could qualify as "the American Bentley" promised top level excitement.

The irony of the Stutz arrival at Le Mans is that it was there because a Stutz had lost to Charles Weymann's Hispano-Suiza in the famous match race a few months before. Weymann nevertheless saw the potential of the Stutz for Le Mans and brought a Series BB Black Hawk back to France to run against the invading Bentleys, ostensibly because he thought it had a better chance than his Hispano. At the time, French cars were conspicuous mostly for their lack of success at Le Mans. Even old Charles Faroux lamented "*C'est une honte!*" . . . "I am ashamed for my own country." So Weymann engaged two French drivers, Robert Bloch and Edouard Brisson, to drive the lone Stutz against the trio of race-proven Bentleys. Amid the carnival *gaieté* which the French blend so well with the serious business of racing, the cars were off; three hours later the excitement of the start was well past and the Stutz settled down to a slight lead. The impeccable Eng-

In 1970 the Stutz name was revived by "Stutz Motor Car of America, Inc." The Stutz of the Seventies uses a modified General Motors chassis fitted with custom coachbuilt Italian body. Like the early Stutz, the car offers a combination of high performance and grand luxury.

COURTESY ENZO STUARTI; PHOTO BY JOHN DURAND, PERMA-TONE STUDIOS

lish gentlemen on hand who had traveled some 350 miles to support the British green seemed even more imperturbable than usual as they adjusted their James Lock bowlers and settled back to wait for what they were sure was the inevitable victory. Everyone knew that cars that rashly went to an early lead were rarely around for the finish. But ten hours later, and even after the mid-way mark, Stutz was still showing the way. The lead was lost briefly after a pit stop but Brisson picked it up again and the betting gentlemen in the crowd began to wonder uneasily about that car from America. By Sunday afternoon they had cause for serious alarm; the lone Stutz had blasted its way through a pair of Bentleys and was now looking down its sights at the third. Only two hours to go before four o'clock.

Woolf Barnato in the Bentley probably couldn't hear it over the din of the race but he surely would have smiled in relief if he had; there was an ominous noise coming from the Stutz. But Brisson heard it, and his reaction was no smile. The overstressed three-speed box in the Stutz was breaking up, and Brisson had to drive with one hand on the lever trying to hold high gear. It was a gallant try by both car and driver, but it was no use and the 4.5-litre Bentley flashed into the record book as the winner.

No car had ever done more to earn second place and despite the last minute bad luck the place position at Le Mans was a resounding victory for the United States. Until 1966, no American car would do as well as that wonderful Stutz. The British and Europeans showed great interest in the Stutz, speculating that it was perhaps the signal of a new American presence in continental racing. Commercially, Stutz did fairly well in the foreign market. An English reporter observed that, "The Americans are establishing themselves on the French market, selling their cars well despite the formidable price handicap of a 67% import duty." However, the success of the Stutz at speed in France probably excited Americans less than anybody else. The majority of U.S. drivers had never heard of Le Mans and probably couldn't have cared less.

The heads that had counseled the carriage trade were—lamentably—closer on target, for Stutz profits were nothing to shout about even at the height of the paper prosperity of the late twenties. But despite the lack of domestic enthusiasm, and perhaps in defiance of it, Stutz was back at Le Mans again in 1929 with the new Model M. This time a proper job was made of the entry. Three Weymann-bodied Speedsters were fitted with supercharged 5.3-litre engines intended to offer up to 155 hp and matched to four-speed gearboxes. But in comparison to Weymann's 1928 "serious amateur" approach, the 1929 effort was a disappointment. When Brisson pulled in for a pit stop somebody got gasoline on hot pipes and the car caught fire, injuring Brisson in the process. The singed car was finally gotten back onto the track but later retired with clutch trouble. The reason for the second Stutz's withdrawal in the small hours of the morning was less dramatic: a split fuel tank. The third car, driven by Bouriat and Phillipe, managed to finish directly behind the procession of four victorious Bentleys. And interestingly, behind the single Stutz came a pair of white American Chryslers, one driven by the great Bugatti driver Roger Benoist.

A few months before the Le Mans disappointment, Fred Moskovics left Stutz, but his philosophies lingered on despite the massing storm clouds on the business horizon. Charles Greuter remained at his post as chief engineer, and to him fell the honor of raising the Stutz to its ultimate glory, the libido-provoking DV-32. The development of the new car continued through 1929 into 1930; it was launched into the bleak 1931 season. In order to meet the increasing demand for power without going to the costly V-12 or even the V-16, which other makers were throwing into the battle against diminishing sales, Greuter discarded the single-overhead cam arrangement, substituted a double-overhead cam, and added two more valves per cylinder. Thus, the sometimes misunderstood "32" referred to the number of valves in the Stutz straight-eight, although there are stories that salesmen would smile agreeably if status-seeking but mechanically naïve customers interpreted this to mean cylinders. The irony of it was that Stutz, like Duesenberg, could do at least as much with eight cylinders as others could with four or even eight more. For all its supposed status, for instance, a V-16 Cadillac would have fallen easy prey to a DV-32 with equal drivers up.

Although the earlier single-overhead-cam engine, still with two valves per cylinder, was retained as the cheaper SV-16, the 32-valve DOHC car became the flagship of the Stutz fleet. Perhaps to capture the popular imagination once again, or

Modern Stutz uses a Pontiac 400 cubic inch V-8 which is torn down and blueprinted to precise specifications, raising compression to 13 to 1 and horsepower from 365 to 425. Singer and auto aficionado Enzo Stuarti took delivery of the first of the new Stutzes.

COURTESY ENZO STUARTI; PHOTO BY JOHN DURAND, PERMA-TONE STUDIOS

maybe just as a last gesture to the Stutz tradition, the venerable name "Bearcat" was trotted out for the roadster version of the DV-32, and it came with an individual factory guarantee that your new Bearcat had done an honest 100 mph on test before you ever slid behind the wheel. For a fortunate few there was the *ne plus ultra* of Stutz automobiles: the short 116-inch-wheelbase, lightweight dream machine called the "Super Bearcat." Discounting the SSJ Duesenberg sports roadsters of kindred spirit (of which only two were built), the Stutz Super Bearcat must surely go down in history as "the great American sports car." And when the Stutz Motor Car Company expired in 1937, the Super Bearcat was its best possible epitaph.

Legends like the Stutz die hard, if at all. More than a generation later, people still recognize the names "Stutz" and "Bearcat," usually in tandem, and they retain much of their old magic. In fact, they still hold enough of it to convince even as conservative a sort as a New York investment broker named James D. O'Donnell that he should form a corporation, sell a million dollars' worth of stock, and spend $250,000 to produce a prototype of a Stutz revival, styled for the 1970s. Economic conditions and the current state of the automotive art do not permit even Wall Streeters to consider conceiving epic automobiles from scratch the way Charles Schwab might have done in the 1920s. Instead, the new "Stutz Motor Car of America, Inc." organization took advantage of what Schwab, Moskovics, and the rest did not have available to them: a fairly cheap but developable stock chassis that can be modified to suit and then fitted out with a line of custom bodies the like of which has not been regularly produced on the North American continent for some time.

The starting point is a Pontiac Grand Prix chassis enriched with Koni adjustable shock absorbers, 17-inch wheels, oversized disc brakes, and Firestone XLL tires. The original 400-cubic-inch V-8 is retained, but torn down and "blueprinted"—reground, modified (including balancing the crankshaft at 17,000 rpm) and reassembled to specifications that increase horsepower from 365 to 425. Then the revised chassis is married to a handbuilt 45-gauge steel body custom-crafted by Carrozzeria Padana in Modena, Italy. Here is where the dollars really show: 22,500 of them for the Blackhawk coupe, $25,000 for a convertible and $29,500 for a formal limousine. In today's inflated economy the prices are hardly more startling than the up to $9000 laid down for an original Stutz in the thirties, although the values received—individuality, craftsmanship and flair—are a bit harder to come by today. Coachwork designs are opulent, well executed and contemporary with a sort of restrained pizazz. The modern management makes no pretense of lineage with the original Stutz, noting that "None of the modern models resemble the original Stutz in any way," although they do describe it as "The car that the designers of the original Stutz might have created if they were designing it today." Perhaps. But in any event it is nice to be able to walk into a showroom and still see a car with the name Stutz on the label.

Chapter 7

THE BRITISH BULLDOG

It is possible to count on the fingers of one hand the number of cars that have made the transition from cold steel to living, breathing things that still cling to life even after their creators have departed it. The British Bentley is one of these hallowed few. To an Englishman a pre-1931 Bentley—one of W.O.'s cars—is nothing less than an emotional experience. It is one thing that can do what Zulu spears, Boers' bullets, or Hitler's rockets could not: ruffle the impervious English calm. Even the stiffest upper lip begins to quiver with emotion when it tells of the greatest moments in English motordom, the epic Bentley battles at Le Mans in the twenties.

Bentley sports cars were hurled down the road to victory and around the curve into legend by an elite group of fanatical followers known as "The Bentley Boys." There were real ones, like a diamond millionaire turned racing driver and an incongruous Harley Street physician who made house calls in a racing Bentley. And there were fictional ones from Bulldog Drummond to James Bond. The Bentley still lured novelists even thirty years after the last one was built. James Bond may hurl his armored Aston-Martin at SPECTRE during office hours, but his pleasanter miles are spent in a vintage Bentley. Ian Fleming, who once appeared on the cover of *Life* in a three-litre, seemed to take special delight in the description of Bond's Bentley in *Casino Royale*. "Bond's car was his only personal hobby. One of the last of the 4½-litre Bentleys with the supercharger by Amherst Villiers, he bought it almost new in 1933 and had kept it in careful storage through the war. It was still serviced every year and, in London, a former Bentley mechanic who worked in a garage near Bond's Chelsea flat, tended it with jealous care. Bond drove it hard and well and with an almost sensual pleasure. It was a battleship grey convertible coupe, which really did convert, and it was capable of touring at ninety with thirty miles an hour in reserve."*

The Bentley story began in those days before World War I when Walter Owen Bentley and his brother ran a small distributorship in London's Hanover Street for a French car called the D.F.P. A few years before, Bentley had picked up the rudiments of mechanical engineering in the shops of the Great Northern railroad, plus a healthy respect for the solid and enduring way that railroad men liked to do things. It was a trait that served him well over the years. After two more years of servicing motor taxis in London, Bentley and his brother pooled their tiny capital and took up business with the little French car in 1912. Although its builders had more conventional ideas in mind, Bentley saw the sturdy two-litre car as a potential sports machine and began to tinker with it. When the adulterated product began to set speed records for its class at over 80 mph, and to win races and hill climbs, Bentley suggested that the D.F.P. initials—which stood for "Doriet Flandrin et Parant"—really meant "deserves first place." When the car finished sixth against some of the most formidable equipment of the day in the rugged 1914 Tourist Trophy run in northern Ireland, Walter Owen Bentley knew that his future lay in building red-blooded automobiles.

That future was somewhat delayed when war swept over

* Used with permission, The Macmillan Company, New York.

Europe a few months after the race through the Irish countryside. When the war came Bentley, unlike Bugatti, Birkigt or Royce, had no organization or manufacturing facilities to produce his designs. But like the others, he turned his talents to air engines and thousands of Bentley-designed rotary engines were ordered, although Captain W.O. Bentley of the Royal Naval Air Service made precious little money out of them. They were advanced in their use of aluminum alloy pistons, an idea that Bentley had tried in the D.F.P. to increase performance and which is supposed to have popped into his head while he was fingering an aluminum piston-shaped paperweight. While W.O. was at Humber's, one of the contractors for his air engines, he met a sympatico engineer named F. T. Burgess. Later, he fell in with Harry Varley who had helped work on the sporting Vauxhalls which had run against Bentley in the Tourist Trophy. The three men shared similar ideas about what sports cars ought to be like, and promised themselves that they would do something about those ideas. Immediately after the Armistice, Bentley, Burgess, and Varley took quarters in a stable in New Street Mews and, as legend has it, the noise of their motors caused considerable irritation among people in a nearby hospital.

Curiously, Bentley never set out to build what many people thought of as a sports car. He did not have in mind a light, stripped and highly tuned machine, but rather a car that was comfortable, reliable and practical as well as fast and well handling: "A car with long legs," as he called it. Beyond his success with the D.F.P. and wartime engine experience, Bentley had also done his homework and looked carefully at Ernest Henry's double-overhead-camshaft Grand Prix Peugeots and at the single-overhead-cam, four-valves-per-cylinder layout of the 1914 Grand Prix Mercedes, one of which was interned in England and available for study. His idea was to bring something of the performance and polish of this kind of machinery down to everyday use—quite a big order by anybody's measure.

A foretaste of the Bentley skill appeared at the great Olympia motor show in November 1919 in the form of a smallish three-litre engine set in a rugged and well balanced chassis. Bentley's display received more than casual glances from the car conscious post-war shoppers, plus a glowing and detailed "review" in *The Autocar*, which called W.O.'s creation "A British super efficient sporting car, the engine of which is designed to keep its 'tune' in the hands of the average owner." The writer leaned heavily on the practical aspects, and with English understatement at work parts of the report seemed to read a little like a Volkswagen ad: ". . . in the hands of the motoring enthusiast . . . able to obtain the last ounce of power from the engine, the car should well repay attention, but the great majority prefer a car which will do its work year in and year out without trouble, and for such is the Bentley designed."

Two months later a finished chassis was fitted with a test body and made available to *The Autocar's* test driver S.C.H. "Sammy" Davis, a name which was to be closely associated with Bentley's over the next decade. For Davis it was love at first sight, and all traces of understatement vanished; he was virtually hypnotized by the new car. At 70 mph he was moved to high emotion, and matching prose: "Every part of one's being urges greater speed in the fierce, wild intoxication of a moment supreme above all others in the life sensations of man."

Davis's ecstasy was appreciated only by a select few during the next year and nine months as the tiny Bentley organization struggled to test and perfect the car and to set up modest manufacturing facilities. In those early days the Bentley operation was very much a shoestring affair and, in fact, never really became "big business." There were frustrating delays, and costs were kept up because many parts had to be farmed out to contractors. But finally the faithful and patient were rewarded with a thin trickle of three-litre Bentleys in

The ultimate Bentley, the great eight-litre. Only about a hundred eight-litres were built, and this is one of the rare short-chassis models fitted with sports coachwork by Corsica. A truly epic car.
BRIGGS CUNNINGHAM AUTOMOTIVE MUSEUM

the autumn of 1921. But those who did wait for one of these firstborn Bentleys got a machine of absolute integrity, enough for Bentley to guarantee it for five years and 80 mph, later raised to 90 mph. These earliest Bentley Boys felt that they got their money's worth, even at about $6000 for a stark sports/tourer, and their loyalty to the struggling young marque was the beginning of the devoted Bentley cult.

Bentley had little budget for advertising his car, but his pre-war D.F.P. experience had taught him that winning races was a surer and ultimately cheaper way of selling sports cars than placing discreet ads in *Country Life*. Some preliminary race testing had been done with experimental cars in 1921 but it was not until the following year that Bentley could really get both feet wet in racing. He got a good bit wet at the R.A.C.'s Tourist Trophy race on the Isle of Man, which was run in a virtual monsoon that year. Bentley entered with a

Proud, imperious, but unpretentious, Bentley stood as a symbol of Britain in the 1920s, and lives on today as one of the best loved sports cars in history.

AUTHOR'S PHOTO

team of three cars, driving one himself, and the others handled by Frank Clement and Douglas Hawkes. The choice of the Tourist Trophy was something of a gallant gesture, for leveled against the little Bentleys like the muzzles of heavy artillery was a team of three Grand Prix-bred Vauxhalls, which held double the Bentley horsepower under their bonnets, plus a pair of racing Sunbeams which also outclassed the Bentleys. The cloudbursts washed out one of the Sunbeams and the much touted Vauxhall threat proved to be a will-o'-the-wisp, two of the three cars dropping out before the end of the race. The surviving Sunbeam went on to win, but the Bentleys took second, fourth, and fifth, the valued team prize, and a very good ladle of publicity.

It is little known that Bentley sent a car to the 1922 Indianapolis "500," although at more expense than the little company could reasonably afford. The car was pretty much outgunned but did the distance with complete reliability at an average of 81 mph. Later that year Bentley reliability was showcased even better on home ground at Brooklands covering 2028 miles in a matched pair of twelve-hour endurance runs, averaging 85 mph. Walter Owen Bentley had his car with long legs.

At about the time Bentley was setting up shop at a satisfyingly English sounding spot called Cricklewood, the French were devising an automotive torture contest almost in the traditions of the Marquis De Sade—*le vingt quatre heures du Mans.* To the 32 cars entered, including one three-litre Bentley, the first Le Mans was an even more formidable challenge than it seems now. The suave, super-highway appearance of today was just a gleam in the eye of Charles Faroux, the organizer of what was to become the world's most famous automobile race. Over frightening roads of dirt, loose gravel, cobblestones, and a few patches of blacktop ran cars of rugged but comparatively unsophisticated suspension, doubtful stopping power (like the Bentley which at the time had rear wheel brakes only), and lighting systems so primitive that the few cars with adequate lights usually had half blind packs of hounds at their heels throughout the night. By comparison, today's Ferraris and Porsches, moving at three times the speed of John Duff's Bentley, probably enjoy at least three times the security and certainly more comfort.

The Bentley works did not officially enter a car in the original Le Mans. Duff's car was his own property although it was works prepared and the co-driver was Frank Clement, Bentley's own test driver. It was Duff who had set the Brooklands Double Twelve endurance record the year before (with the same car) and, as a Bentley dealer, saw the commercial value of appearing at Le Mans. There was also the question of showing the flag, since Duff's would be the only British car in the race. The Bentley promptly set up some very rapid laps and gave every promise of going the full distance. Loose gravel was a frightful hazard at the premier Le Mans, and it was especially costly to Bentley. Machine gun-like hails of stones were kicked up and pelted the cars and drivers without mercy. Virtually everything made of glass was shattered, and the Bentley fuel tank and gas line were also hit. But despite its injuries the lone Bentley plowed on and managed fourth place among the twenty-eight finishers.

Duff was back again at the Sarthe circuit for the following year's race. This time the green, tub-shaped Bentley withstood the worst that the course could throw at it (only 14 of 41 cars finished) and Duff brought his three-litre home in first place to open "the Bentley years" at Le Mans. In five years the Bentley had risen from a gleam in its creator's eye to the cream of sports car racing. England and the world were noticing Bentleys, and buying them.

At the time of the first Le Mans victory Bentley had to meet the market with only his three-litre, although this model was ultimately available in as many as six varieties. First, there was the original production car which began delivery in 1921. The following year a replica of the Isle of Man Tourist Trophy car was offered with a hotter, 90-mph engine. The most popular of the three-litres was the "Long Standard" chassis which added thirteen inches of wheelbase to the original 117½

A 1926 three-litre with a boat tail body, so typical of sporting tastes in the mid-1920s, this one with a wooden planked rear deck to complete the nautical theme. Body is by Vanden Plas which clothed many of the Cricklewood chassis.

BRIGGS CUNNINGHAM AUTOMOTIVE MUSEUM

inches. This model accounted for about half of the 1600 or so three-litres built. The next most numerous was the famous "red label" or Speed Model three-litre with the original short wheelbase and a high compression engine. The so-called "red label" designation, which was never encouraged by the factory, referred to the fact that the enameled background of the winged "B" emblem carried on the radiator was changed to red from blue as used on the original model, Tourist Trophy, and Long Standard cars. Such a color-change occurred again in the three-litre series on the rare "100 mph" model introduced in 1925 with a shortened 108-inch wheelbase and a still higher compression engine. Only 15 such exotic three-litres were built and they carried green enamel insignia. The full three-litre catalogue is completed with the "Light Tourer," the least expensive of the type.

Despite the six "flavors" of the three-litre, it became obvious by the middle twenties that Bentley needed a larger car.

In its present form the car was fairly well limited to light, open sports bodies. Some customers fitted more commodious bodies for extended touring and a few used closed bodies. Performance declined quickly under the added weight and became very un-Bentley. Cricklewood's answer came in 1926 in the form of a six-cylinder 6.5-litre, the so-called "Big Six." Again, Bentley most certainly did not set out to build a sports car but simply updated his concept of the car with long legs in order to meet increasing demands. This he did quite well, producing a smooth and much more flexible car capable of carrying sports sedan or even limousine coachwork in speedy silence. The chassis price rose to $7250, but Bentley could now successfully compete in the carriage class where price was no great barrier.

Bentley's venture into the luxury field was by no means a slight to the marque's essence as a sports machine. Racing was carried on with the usual enthusiasm and Bentleys appeared in strength at the 1925 Le Mans. In just two years the "twenty-four hours" had developed into a popular sporting spectacle that attracted thousands of spectators. This year, for the first time, they saw forty-nine drivers in the frantic scramble that became famous as the "Le Mans start." Somewhere among the potpourri of national colors and bluish exhaust haze was a pair of British racing green three-litre Bentleys, for the first time an official factory-entered team. One of the cars driven by the experienced John Duff and Frank Clement was forced out with fuel line and carburetor problems. The other was driven by Kensington Moir and Dr. J. Dudley Benjafield. Moir was a professional driver, but Benjafield was one of the Bentley Boys. Descending the front steps of a patient's Georgian townhouse, he was quite the proper English consultant, with black leather medical case and sombre Homburg to match. But this staid image was brutally shattered when he climbed into his three-litre at the curb and disappeared behind a barrage of exhaust noises. The Moir-Benjafield entry had its work cut out for it against the five twin-cam Sunbeams which were making their premier appearance, and for a time there was a lively fight between the rival Britons. But ultimately it was something as "trivial" as a fuel miscalculation that left number 10 Bentley marooned along the course and disqualified.

The middle twenties were tumultuous times for Bentley. The three-litre was being developed to its final form; the "Big Six" 6.5-litre was in production and buyers were beginning to ask for a warmed-up sports version of it; a successor to the obsolescent three-litre was in the works; and on top of it all, time and imagination had to be found to convince creditors that the world occasionally turns on things other than money. The Bentley organization was never one to operate with anything like cool efficiency, and it is to the enormous credit of W.O. Bentley that he was able to create such great machines in a state of constant crisis. For him there was

Just 50 blown 4.5-litre Bentleys were built at the urging of Sir Henry Birkin but against W.O. Bentley's inclinations. The supercharged car's great appeal was its basic, gut-level function-over-form character, plus a look of absolute menace.

AUTHOR'S PHOTO

A magnificent "Speed Six" with a Weymann type fabric body by Vanden Plas and the big 6.5-litre engine.
BRIGGS CUNNINGHAM AUTOMOTIVE MUSEUM

neither a Molsheim to restore the spirit nor the treasury of a General Motors to absorb miscalculation.

Bentleys were never anything other than expensive cars. The "Light Tourer" three-litre at about $5000 was the cheapest, and a full Grand Prix Bugatti chassis could be had for less than the cost of some Bentleys. Nevertheless, they sold comparatively well. For instance, the 1600 three-litres sold was quite a respectable record for an expensive sports car of the twenties; and about a third of them survive today. But very little of the Bentley's stiff price represented profit, and the little company at Cricklewood struggled continually to keep its head above the waves.

The year 1926 might well have been the last for Bentley if it had not been for one of the Bentley Boys. Woolf Barnato was heir to a South African diamond fortune who would not see the producer of one of his favorite amusements fall into oblivion for the lack of—to him—a trifling sum. An injection of pounds sterling into the firm's veins gave it new life, and to Barnato chairmanship of the board of directors plus an even more highly prized seat—a place on the Bentley team.

The stay of execution gave W.O. a breathing spell to create

what the Bentley Boys were clamoring for, a new sports car to supplant the outgunned three-litre. His answer was the 4.5-litre, which consisted basically of a Big Six engine with two of the cylinders chunked out; so the interchangeability of some of the parts between the two 100 x 140 mm bore and stroke engines could ease production problems a little. Recalling that W.O. Bentley spent his teenage years in the shops of the Great Northern and looking at the battleship bulk of the 4.5-litre, you couldn't help feeling that locomotives still pleased him. But she was a crack train, her cylinders, each of more than one litre, pumping out a flow of smooth, sure power to give an honest hundred without tuning the car within an inch of its life. In racing trim she was perhaps homely—did not Ettore Bugatti say that "Monsieur Bentley builds very fast trucks?"—but she was something you could believe in. Englishmen did believe, and have ever since.

With the new 4.5-litre, Bentley intended to give all out battle in the 1927 Le Mans. (A trio of three-litres had fought well the year before but had to settle for fifth, seventh and eighth places.) One of the earliest 4.5-litres was entered, to be driven by veteran Frank Clement and Leslie Callingham, plus a pair of three-litres from the 1926 race, one of them Dr. Benjafield's car now nicknamed "Old Number Seven." Benjafield's co-driver would be S.C.H. "Sammy" Davis, automotive writer and charter member of the Bentley Boys, and the other three-litre would be shared between Baron D'Erlanger and George Duller, a horseman turned sports car fan. At four in the afternoon the three Bentleys led the pack away from the scrambling start and were followed down the road by nineteen other cars, one of the smallest fields to race at Le Mans. Frank Clement led in the 4.5-litre, Dr. Benjafield was second, and the Baron D'Erlanger brought up the rear of the Bentley triumvirate. In the slowly failing light of the longest day and on into the evening they sped in neat 1-2-3 order, with Clement taking a lap record at 73 mph in the 4.5.

As night reluctantly settled over the twenty-two cars they began to pull into the pits for driver changes. Clement climbed

out of the lead car and the leather was then warmed by Leslie G. Callingham who was driving his first Le Mans in a Bentley. The doctor was replaced by Sammy Davis, and George Duller took over from the Baron. For non-Bentley fans the race had been almost mechanical up to this time. Places rarely changed hands and swans gliding over a pond would have provided nearly as much excitement.

Maps and charts of the Le Mans course show a fairly innocent wiggle in the road that looks not nearly as formidable as the infamous Pontlieue hairpin. But actually it was an awkward blind bend which has grown infamous as "the White House Corner," so called for a quaint little French farmhouse at the roadside. About 9:30 P.M. a small French Schneider headed into this curve with the driver's foot pressed down a little too firmly. At the last moment he lost control and crashed, spreading debris over the road. Seconds later Leslie Callingham came up in the 4.5 at nearly eighty and by the time he saw what had happened it was too late to do anything but pull the wheel and pray. As Callingham regained his senses he was aware of three things: a bloody nose, a badly smashed 4.5-litre, and the lights of another car rushing into White House. The lights belonged to a French Fasto and they caught the scene just in time for the driver to stand on his brakes. The Fasto screamed and squealed, lurched and pranced through the wreckage and then turned completely around to face George Duller rushing up in his three-litre. To avoid the still percolating Fasto, Duller chose the same ditch where Callingham's 4.5 was lying and the two Bentleys met with a resounding crash. And it still wasn't over. Sammy Davis in "Old Number Seven" was next into White House, picking up the

In order to show that the post-Bentley Bentleys were not the foppish cars that their critics were claiming, Rolls-Royce, Ltd. permitted a very restrained racing program which demonstrated the Rolls-Bentleys as quite worthy descendents of W.O.'s cars. This 4.5-litre, works prepared for race driver E. R. Hall, was one of the cars which provided the proof.

BRIGGS CUNNINGHAM AUTOMOTIVE MUSEUM

A beautifully restored 3.5-litre Bentley coupe, body by Park Ward.
AUTHOR'S PHOTO

Fasto's skid marks soon enough to brake. His alert reaction was a help, but not enough. In a masterpiece of evasive steering, he avoided everything but the tail of Callingham's car and he hit that with a bone-jarring crash. If there was ever a time for the legendary Bentley solidity to prove itself this was it. Unhurt, Davis nursed the grievously wounded little three-litre down the road to the pits where an assessment of the damage was made. The right front fender was bent nearly across the hood, the wheel under it was virtually destroyed, and the axle on which it rode was bent. The battery hung precariously from the running board mount, and one headlight plus the auxiliary light was gone.

"Old Number Seven" and Bentley's high hopes were both a sorry mess. Davis's insistence that the car could still compete was gallant but it seemed useless. There were still nearly eighteen hours to go and a powerful French Aries had snatched the lead and was running strong. But Davis prevailed. A strong arm and mall dealt with the smashed fender, the damaged wheel was replaced and the dangling battery lashed

A very unusual dual cowl sports phaeton by the Dutch coach-builders Vesters & Neirinck on a 4.5-litre Bentley chassis.

MR. JOHN C. NORTH II, ESQ.

back into place with wire. An emergency lamp went on with wire, tar tape and an oath or two. The bent axle could only be prayed over. A half hour later Davis gamely shot off into the night with the husky Bentley engine roaring defiance. Shortly, the sky opened up in torrents to make the French night even more unfriendly.

Sunrise found the Bentley still slinging mud with Davis and Dr. Benjafield still spelling each other at the wheel. But the French Aries still had a 40-mile lead. If the British are at their best in times of adversity, now was the time to prove it. So, as Benjafield passed the pits, he was not surprised to see W.O. Bentley anxiously signaling for speed. He smiled and stepped up the pace until the jury rigged three-litre seemed to be flying. Gradually, the Aries' 40 miles began to dwindle and the clock hand began to edge toward four. Still the broken but unbowed Bentley came on to dog the heels of the Aries, and the French team's smiles began to evaporate. By early afternoon only half a lap separated the hunter and the hunted. The hair stood up on the backs of English necks craning to see from the roadsides if Britannia would rule the road that day. But the grind had been too much, and an overstressed camshaft gave way only minutes from the end—the camshaft in the Aries! The muddy, battered British green car was home first. There would be other Bentley wins at Le Mans, but not quite like this one. It was a moment of emotion and victory that stood with Wellington at Waterloo and Nelson at Trafalgar.

It was also a moment of English sportsmanship and courtesy. With minutes remaining, Dr. Benjafield made one more stop and called for Davis to take over. It was, he reasoned, Davis's victory and he should be the one to take the flag. He did, and behind him were 1472 hard-fought miles and only seven other survivors.

In 1928 another new Bentley appeared, the inevitable sports version of the 6.5-litre, christened the "Speed Six" and carrying a green label on its radiator in place of the standard blue. Basically, the new sports car retained the Big Six engine but in a modified form. The old 4.4:1 compression ratio was upped to 5.3 (5.5 in some):1 (6.1:1 in the Le Mans type), a new camshaft was added and more attention given to valves, bringing horsepower up to 180 at 3500 rpm and to 200 hp in the Le Mans type. For its increased performance the Speed Six yielded none of its flexibility and polish; in fact, it showed Bentley's increasing skill for the class *de grand luxe*. In April 1929 *The Motor* took a big, heavy Gurney-Nutting-bodied sedan out around Brooklands track at 90 mph and reported that "A conversation could be carried on with the other occupants of the car without the slightest difficulty." They also reported a minimum speed of only 4 mph in top gear, demonstrating the amazing flexibility of the engine.

In 1928 Bentley was back at Le Mans with a team of 4.5-litres pitted against an expanded field which included the formidable American Stutz eight-cylinder. The benefactor and chairman of the Bentley board of directors, Woolf Barnato, was on the team this time with the very same car that had been smashed at White House the year before. His famous duel with the Black Hawk Stutz right up to the last minutes of the twenty-four-hours provided the same sort of edge-of-the-seat excitement that Sammy Davis and Dr. Benjafield had supplied the year before and gave Barnato the first of his grand string of wins at Le Mans.

A quartet of Bentleys descended on Le Mans in 1929, one of them a Speed Six bolstered by three trusty 4.5-litres. The competition promised to be stiff: a trio of well prepared Stutz speedsters and a pair of Chryslers from America; a more enthusiastic British presence in the form of Alvis, Invicta, Lagonda, and Lea-Francis teams; an unusual eight-piston, four-cylinder, two-stroke Tracta, and more. But once the race was under way it was, from the spectators' seats at least, a routine run without the high drama of the last two races. Sans spectacle, the four Bentleys led by Sir Henry Birkin in the Speed Six circled the course with the detached composure of orbiting satellites and a day later came home in the same 1-2-3-4 drill order in which they had started.

Like Andre Dubonnet and his love affair with the Hispano-Suiza, Sir Henry Birkin was devoted to Bentleys and eventually, like Dubonnet, set out to improve upon what seemed near perfection. It was Sir Henry's idea that the sparkle of the 4.5-litre could be enhanced by supercharging the hearty four-cylinder engine. Like Ettore Bugatti, W.O. Bentley was aghast at the thought, sharing Bugatti's philosophy that supercharging—to be polite—cast an aura of illegitimacy over his design. But eventually Birkin wore Bentley down to mere reluctance, and an obliging millionairess named Miss Dorothy Paget agreed to finance the noble experiment. The lady's money bought exactly fifty supercharged Bentleys, a living legend, and not very much more.

Despite the folklore surrounding the blown Bentley, it never did anything particularly spectacular. In fact, quite unlike the "ordinary" 4.5-litre, it never won a major race. When some of the cars were offered for sale, the advertisements listing "1930 performances" contained a fairly lacklustre list of accomplishments, although the guarantee of 125 mph was enticing. But the blown Bentley's great strength was its appearance, particularly as the classic, four-seater, open Vanden Plas tourer. It was possessed in abundance with that basic, gut-level function-over-form character common to all timeless automobiles, plus a look of absolute menace exceeded only by that of certain types of Mercedes-Benz. A blown 4.5 looked very fast—and very mean—just standing cold at curbside.

The blown 4.5 is instantly recognizable from all other Bentleys at a glance—it is not hard to spot a car with a massive supercharger and carburetor plopped smack out in front of everything at the base of the radiator! Like the headlights, the vulnerable parts were shielded by a heavy wire mesh stoneguard. This arrangement hardly made for svelte elegance, but it seemed to give the blown 4.5 a unique aura of virility. The blower was a Roots type, by Amherst Villiers, that could give up to ten pounds pressure per square inch. As a practical matter it did a lot to smooth out the big four-cylinder engine.

Attractive drop head coupe on the 3.5-litre Rolls-Bentley chassis of 1933, advertised as "the silent sports car."

COURTESY ROLLS-ROYCE, LTD.

Sir Henry's pet project had its closest brush with great victory in the 1930 Le Mans when it fought a bitter duel with a lone supercharged seven-litre 38/250 Mercedes-Benz under command of Rudolf Caracciola. The upshot of this esoteric combat was simply that Birkin and Caracciola wore each other down until finally both cars went out and left the way clear for a pair of Bentley Speed Sixes to take first and second. The victory that year went to Woolf Barnato, his third (consecutive) win at Le Mans, and Bentley's fifth—and last. It was an exciting finale for the Bentley years at Le Mans for, in the face of the financial terror that was upon the world, the firm decided to retire from racing. With five wins out of eight appearances at Le Mans alone between 1923 and 1930, plus its other assorted successes, it could afford to do so with unquestioned honor. The English record in France would be approached by Jaguar in the 1950s, but somehow the glamor of Bentley at Le Mans in the twenties could never quite be matched.

There was yet another Bentley, and it was in the most troubled times of all that this ultimate car came from Cricklewood. The great eight-litre which was born against the bleak background of 1930 was the final expression of the Bentley philosophy of the car with long legs. Like his first little three-litre, the last Bentley was not intended as a sports car (a not unchallenged claim) but as a very comfortable car which could also be driven very fast. Toward his particular goal, Walter Owen Bentley succeeded perhaps better than any other designer. *The Motor* examined the eight-litre, quoted a dictionary definition of "unique" as "single in its kind of excellence," and then said "In this sense and without qualification the new eight-litre Bentley is a unique car."

And it was. You could drive to any address, anywhere, and be socially secure, or over any road at virtually any speed and be physically secure. To accomplish this, Bentley had devised a 7.98-litre, six-cylinder engine of kinship to the Speed Six, and placed it into a massive, well braced twelve- or thirteen-foot chassis which reflected all those years of race-bred expertise. The engine could calmly offer 220 hp at 3500 rpm, with more available, and the torque was so great that the car would walk along at five or six mph in top gear and then accelerate from 10 to 100 in 50 seconds without the bother of changing gears. Comfort and tractability amazed everyone who drove the car, and one test driver observed that "one gains the impression that all four wheels are definitely biting the road and are likely to continue to do so." And on top of it all there was Rolls-Royce-style silence, which incidentally created some formidable competition for the flying lady since there was nothing in the Rolls-Royce catalogue at the moment which could hold its own with an opened up eight-litre. Yet the Bentley could successfully challenge the Rolls for refinement and luxury.

In building his car, Bentley claimed that he had no interest in weight-saving since he wasn't building an all-out high per-

Sports sedan by Vanvooren on the 4.5-litre Rolls-Bentley chassis.
COURTESY ROLLS-ROYCE, LTD.

formance car, and a sports sedan version of the eight-litre weighed in at some 6000 pounds. However, a few purchasers (there were only about a hundred in all) ordered two-seater sports bodies on the twelve-foot chassis and found themselves with anything but town carriage characteristics. The most famous of these belonged to a gentleman named Forrest Lycett who developed and modified the car much as the company itself might have done, say in the fashion of the Big Six maturing into the Speed Six. With this machine, acceleration on the order of 0 to 100 mph in 18 seconds, and speeds like 140 mph (as recorded on the Jabbeke-Ostend highway in 1950 with a twenty-year-old car) were possible.

An aura of intrigue still surrounds the collapse of Bentley Motors, Ltd in the summer of 1931. Apparently, another transfusion by Barnato or by another of the marque's millionaire friends could have seen it over the rough spots, for the company was finally beginning to make money. It cleared a profit of over $125,000 in 1929 and the eight-litre could have developed into a fine money maker. Bentley himself said that an eight-litre could be built for not much more than a three-litre yet yielded nearly five times the profit. But the die was cast and this time no one rushed to the rescue. Instead, the company tried to stave off disaster by cutting corners. The magnificent eight-litre engine was a gem, but a very costly one. So, the firm commissioned Sir Harry Ricardo to design a less expensive four-litre, pushrod, six-cylinder which could be installed on the eight-litre chassis. Both components were good in their own spheres, but together they were a sad mismatch. In today's terms it would be roughly comparable to putting a Mercedes economy diesel in a Mercedes 600 limousine. The move knocked about $3000 off the chassis price—and worlds off the appeal of the car. Sadly, the four-litre failed as both a car and a policy maneuver; it appeared in May of 1931 and the company went into receivership in July.

When a receiver offered the Bentley assets on the market an interested bidder came up with something over half a million dollars in pocket. It was Napier & Son, Ltd which had built high quality luxury cars earlier in the century and then retired from the field to concentrate on airplane engines. Napier saw the eight-litre for what it was: the masterwork of a great designer. He also saw the chance to re-enter the automobile business with one of the very best motorcars ever built. However, the constructors of "the world's best car" took a dim view of this, and in a dramatic eleventh hour *coup d'etat* Rolls-Royce bought out Bentley Motors, Ltd and quietly slipped the eight-litre into an unmarked grave.

Messrs Rolls-Royce, Ltd did not, however, dispense with the magic of the Bentley name quite so summarily. On the one hand the name "Bentley" had become a matter of national pride, and on the other it still held no small commercial value. So, when Rolls-Royce undertook to manufacture Bentley cars it wisely acquired the services of W.O. Bentley to assist in the project. At first there were some experiments with a small supercharged engine, vaguely reminiscent of the blown 4.5-litre, but this proved unsatisfactory and the project turned to a modified version of the stock 20/25 engine of the "baby Rolls." The modifications consisted primarily of raising the compression ratio from 5.7:1 to 6.5:1 and improving carburetion. After some teething problems were ironed out in the earliest cars, what emerged was a very desirable car that was at once polished, practical, and pretty. The "Rolls-Bentleys"—to distinguish them from "Bentley Bentleys"—have been called "the silent sports cars" and in fact the company literature promised that "Performance and Peace can now be reconciled," an advertising phrase which, on reflection, seems remarkably modern. Evidently, what the Rolls-Royce hierarchy envisioned was a car that would marry Rolls silence and sophistication to Bentley spirit, a seemingly improbable marriage but a very nice one if it could be brought off.

When the "new Bentleys" appeared in 1933 not a few "old Bentley" fans were at first convinced that it was a marriage headed for divorce. The old "fire breather" feel of the 4.5-litre was gone and in its place was an unsupercharged 3.5-litre chassis (based on a touring car!) clad in svelte and elegant sports/touring bodies or closed four-door sedans, often from Vanden Plas, the same coachbuilder responsible for the battle cruiser Bentleys. But when the critics looked closer they could still find what had always been behind the winged "B"—a car with long legs. In 1936 the legs grew a bit longer with the coming of a 4.25-litre engine. And as much as one might miss the "old Bentleys" it was hard to find fault with the "new Bentleys" which carried some strikingly beautiful and proportionate lines. Ettore Bugatti's observation about trucks now held water like a sieve.

Rolls-Royce was breaking down the barriers in offering something as frivolous as a "sporting car." The closest they had come since James Radley's "Alpine Eagle" of pre-World War I days was the rare Phantom II Continental of 1934, "a fast touring car." And more was coming. When a very satisfied customer (and race driver) named E. H. Hall asked the company to sanction his 3.5-litre Bentley for the 1934 Tourist Trophy race—wonder of wonders—dispensation from Derby was granted, and factory facilities were even made available to "works prepare" Hall's car, which afterward delivered 130 hp (up from 110) and 110 mph (up from about 90 mph). Hall finished second against stiff competition and, to reply to critics, returned a better average speed than the blown 4.5-litre had under similar conditions. For 1935 Hall repeated the performance, as before losing first place by handicap only.

Through the thirties, development continued on the Bentley and speeds reached 112 mph and 114 mph (the latter for a steady hour at Brooklands track). An aerodynamic, but not very pretty, body design called the "Corniche" was created in Paris for a new chassis with independent front suspension but few of either had been built when the war intervened. Reportedly, a few were fitted with an experimental straight-eight, 5.5-litre engine. It was this Bentley, known as the Mark V, which began to draw away from the sporting car concept and which set the stage for the more sedate post-war Bentleys. An era was finally ending, but at least it had been postponed by a very worthwhile ten-year reprieve.

Chapter 8

La DOLCE VETTURA: ALFA ROMEO

The world would be a sorry place if it were not for the Italians. Their gifts to art and music, not to mention food, and the uniquely Italian celebration of the joy of living, all rate high in the catalogue of human accomplishment. Certainly the world of automobiles would be a good deal poorer if it were not for the imprint that the Italian touch has made on motorcars, and is still making.

One of the fascinating things about cars is how they have tended to reflect the prominent national characteristics of their creators: the English refinement and good manners of the Rolls-Royce; the German technical expertise and pursuit of perfection in the Mercedes-Benz; the French love of line, style, and *panache* in the Hispano-Suiza; the American preoccupation with power, price and prestige in the Duesenberg. Italian cars have had their share of these qualities, but their one grand virtue is a pure *felicita di vita* which no other machine is quite able to duplicate. To gather together a scenic road, an attractive companion, and an Italian sports car is to know one of life's exquisite joys. Being Latin, the car is entitled to a measure of temperament, and can teach you the meaning of exaspera-

One of the earliest sports-racing ALFAS, a 15/20 hp of 1913. Top speed was 65 mph.

ALFA ROMEO

A prestigious technical accomplishment for young ALFA, the 4.5-litre, double-overhead-camshaft Grand Prix car, the first from Italy. Chief engineer Giuseppe Merosi is at the wheel, with his engineer Faragiana on his left.

ALFA ROMEO

tion. But when she has been sufficiently soothed, praised, and loved and the mood is on her, she is on your side like no other car on the road. If cars can be considered a stimulant—and they certainly should be—then one probably gets higher highs and lower lows from Italian machines than from any other breed.

If there is one car that typifies the best of the Italian way with automobiles, it is Alfa Romeo. ALFAs have not had quite the stubborn individuality of Bugattis, although a rationale which once conceived a car with twin engines one before and the other behind the driver, and a racer with both right and left hand gear shift levers to suit the driver's choice could hardly be called conventional. But the company's normal willingness to do things with less self sufficiency than their expatriate countryman at Molsheim (but hardly with less grace) did

The 4.2-litre Alfa Romeo known as the ES Sport represented a marriage of pre- and post-war efforts. Running in the Targa Florio and other Italian races, the car laid the groundwork for Alfa Romeo's great racing success between the wars.

ALFA ROMEO

Catalogue image of the ES Sport looked almost Edwardian and quite dated for 1921, reflecting its 1910 ancestry. But more exciting things were on the way.

ALFA ROMEO

not detract a bit from the charisma which has grown up around ALFAs. Even old Henry Ford is once reported to have said, "I take off my hat when I see an Alfa Romeo go by."

It is an interesting coincidence that the first ALFAs and the first Bugattis were under construction at exactly the same time, January 1910. But beyond sharing a birthday, the two marques had little in common, at least in the beginning. The first Bugatti was born as the inspiration of one man's mind and his artistic dedication to his cause; ALFA's origins were more commercial and conventional. The French Darracq company had set up an assembly plant near Milan in 1906 to cater to the Italian market, but the project was not a success and some local entrepreneurs bought out the interest, founded the "(Societa) Anonima Lombarda Fabbrica Automobili," and added another of those beloved Italian automotive acronyms to an already growing list—ALFA.

Ugo Sivocci at the wheel of the RLTF in which he won the 1923 Targa Florio. The RL series sports cars were the beginning of the Alfa Romeo tradition of fine handling, high performance sports cars of modest displacement. The "four leaf clover" racing insignia on the nose first rode on the RL cars and has ridden with Alfa Romeo racers ever since.

ALFA ROMEO

Unlike Bugatti, the new company's businessmen founders had no specific ideas in mind about what their product should be like. So, an automotive designer of proven merit named Giuseppe Merosi was brought in and set to work creating the first ALFA. The car was a big four-cylinder, displacing one litre for each cylinder, and could give up to 60 mph. Merosi also did a "baby brother" version of the car which was nearly as fast with about half the displacement, and it was this car which became the first sports/racing ALFA. The standard production chassis fitted out for the Targa Florio offered the usual profile of the era: hooded engine with steering wheel

The 1924 Targa Florio was well attended, with 37 entries. Here, Andre Boillot with his sleeve-valve four-litre Peugeot gives battle to the Alfa Romeo team. Mercedes won that year, with Alfa Romeo RLTF cars second and third.

AUTOMOBILES PEUGEOT

and controls jutting out from the dashboard, traces of a pair of seats backed with a steel cylinder of gasoline, and a rear mounted spare.

Enthusiasm burned brightly for the new company and Merosi was kept busy at his drawing board turning out new ALFA designs. Among them was the first Italian double-over-head-camshaft Grand Prix car. Even though the car did not make it to the 1914 French Grand Prix, where it is likely that it would have been chewed up with the rest of the victims of the Mercedes meat grinder, it was still a prestigious accomplishment for the little four-year-old company. However, fortunes did not shine as brightly for young ALFA as its enthusiasm

A 1925 RLSS fitted with sporty boat tail body, the rakish Vee-radiator which was the badge of the type, and pointed windscreen to match.

ALFA ROMEO

and shortly the company was caught up in the turmoil of World War I, absorbed into the industrial empire of Nicola Romeo and set to cranking out mostly war materiel.

Fortunately, however, Nicola Romeo had a flamboyant Italian love of automobiles and saw ALFA as more than figures on a balance sheet. Quite a bit more. As soon as peace broke out ALFA became Alfa Romeo, immediately concerned itself with the design and construction of first rate motorcars, and promptly fell into the thick of racing them. The early Alfa Romeos were understandably related to the pre-war ALFAs, and the two regimes merged well. One issue of the marriage of pre-war ALFA and post-war Alfa Romeo was a 4.2-litre,

Moving stylishly in the 1920s on the Italian peninsula meant owning an RLSS Alfa Romeo.

ALFA ROMEO

Vittorio Jano's triumph, the P2 Alfa Romeo. The car was the brightest star of the 1924 season, taking virtually everything there was to be had in motor racing. With the P2, Alfa Romeo became a power in the racing world and the red cars carrying the cross and serpent of the arms of Milano would always have to be reckoned with wherever fast cars gathered.

ALFA ROMEO

80-mph sports model which traced its ancestry all the way back to the original ALFA of 1910. With the ES Sport and another hybrid car Alfa Romeo began to make its presence known on Italian race circuits.

The early and middle twenties were busy times for Alfa Romeo: designing, testing, building, racing, and selling. In 1922 the company offered the first of the RL series, the first of the "glamour" Alfa Romeos. In original form the RL didn't seem so glamorous: a three-litre, six-cylinder touring car of average performance, indifferent stopping ability, and a valve gear that had to be lubricated by hand every thousand miles or so. At a bare chassis price of about $3000, it hardly seemed a glamorous bargain either. However, it was not the first time, nor would it be the last, that a fine sports car was developed out of a tame touring car. The caterpillar blossomed into the

The infamous P1, Alfa Romeo's star-crossed car. The car was said to be dangerously unstable and one of Alfa Romeo's great drivers, Ugo Sivocci, was killed in a P1 practicing for the 1923 Italian Grand Prix at Monza.

ALFA ROMEO

butterfly in the sports version, known as the RLSS or the 22/90 hp. Completing the metamorphosis was a striking vee-shaped radiator grille, and the fitting of handsome two- and four-seater sports/touring bodies in the jaunty boat tailed styles of the 1920s. But there was more to the RLSS cars than just a visual face lifting. If there were any doubts about that they were resolved by the RLTF, a version of the RL cars specially groomed for the 1923 Targa Florio. After a hard day's run through the Sicilian mud and mountains Alfa Romeo had captured first, second, and fourth places, and the "TF" in the title letters was there for good cause shown.

In the 6C 1750 *Gran Sport* Vittorio Jano distilled the very essence of a great sports car. The 1750 Alfa Romeo represented a delicate balance of art and engineering, of beauty and practicality. It has justly gone down into history as one of the great cars of all time.
ALFA ROMEO

As the Alfa Romeo star began to rise, Giuseppe Merosi set to work designing a double-overhead-cam Grand Prix car to comply with the two-litre formula in then effect, but somewhere along the way it became a star crossed quest. Writers have indicated that the chassis was unstable at speed, and this may have well been the case for one of Alfa Romeo's top drivers and winner of the 1923 Targa Florio, Ugo Sivocci, was killed when his P1 GP car missed a curve at Monza in practice for the 1923 Italian Grand Prix. In any case, Alfa Romeo immediately abandoned the P1.

The 1750 was more than just a pleasant, pretty sports car. On the race tracks of Europe it was a tiger. In a single season it won the Grand Prix races of Belgium, Spain, Rome, Tunis, and Monza, plus the Ulster Tourist Trophy, the Mille Miglia, and the Double Twelve race of Brooklands.

ALFA ROMEO

A 6C 1750 *Gran Turismo* (DOHC) fitted with an interesting closed coupe body and prepared for racing.

ALFA ROMEO

The powers at Alfa Romeo decided that a little new blood in the drawing office might not be a bad idea, and it arrived from the FIAT organization in the person of Vittorio Jano who was assigned to do something about the ill-fated Monza Grand Prix car project. At this point an interesting parallel occurs in the history of Alfa Romeo and Mercedes. At about the same time, Daimler's was having problems with its own two-litre, double-cam Grand Prix car, and one of the greatest names in classic auto sport, Count Louis Zborowski, was killed at Monza in the Italian Grand Prix in this Mercedes the year after Sivocci was killed in the Alfa Romeo. At the crucial moment an Austrian engineer named Ferdinand Porsche arrived at Daimler's to fix the two-litre GP car and opened one of Mercedes' epic eras with a series of great cars from his drawing board. Porsche came to Stuttgart in spring 1923; Jano to Milan in the winter of the same year. Like Porsche, Jano masterfully resolved the GP car problem and, like Porsche, opened a grand epoch for his marque with a series of brilliant cars.

Instead of revising the P1, Jano created a wholly new car, the P2, a double-overhead-cam straight-eight fitted with a Roots type supercharger which ultimately offered 156 hp at 5500 rpm and nearly 140 mph. Working under the spectre of the P1, Jano's attention to the chassis was precise and meticulous (as was his attention to anything he did) and the P2 ran as if welded to the road. It had the feel of a winner. That feel would be vindicated and then some in the 1924 season when the P2 mopped up just about everything in sight, including the brand new Type 35 Bugatti at the French Grand Prix, which fell victim to bad tires as le Patron sat and watched his beautiful little blue cars drive to defeat on disintegrating rubber. At the Italian Grand Prix that year the P2 finished 1-2-3-4. Alfa Romeo had arrived. From that time on, the blood-red cars carrying the cross and serpent of the arms of Milano would always have to be reckoned with wherever fast cars gathered.

While the P2 was carrying Alfa Romeo to glory on the racing circuits there were some new rumblings on the sports scene. A new Alfa Romeo sports car known technically as the 6C 1500 and popularly as the *Turismo* was announced in 1926. It began not only a dynasty of cars but also a philosophy which resulted in what might be called *la dolce vettura* for its joyous driving qualities. The new car was a 1.5-litre, single-overhead-cam, six-cylinder machine, meticulously crafted and finished and ostensibly intended as a touring car. But, like the RL series before it, that was not to be its fate. Soon the 6C 1500 Sports—the *Gran Turismo*—(Alfa Romeo seems to have been the first to use this now overworked title) appeared with the 1.5-litre block now fitted with a double-overhead cam, and

The 6C 1750 as it appeared in the 1931 Mille Miglia, which was won that year by Rudolf Caracciola with an SSK Mercedes-Benz, the first of only two times in history when the event was won by a non-Italian car.

ALFA ROMEO

89
ASSICURATRICE
AUTOMOBILI
GENOVA

In 1929 an Alfa Romeo driver named Enzo Ferrari founded the *Scuderia Ferrari* to race Alfa Romeos. Here, Ferrari (far left) with Tazio Nuvolari's hand on his shoulder smiles after a victory.

ALFA ROMEO

Much of Alfa Romeo's success was due to the great drivers who drove the red cars from Milano. Here, Nuvolari–the "Flying Mantuan"–and Bonini share an Alfa.

ALFA ROMEO

a few competition specimens with superchargers. Aside from the lively performance and Swiss-watch construction, the outstanding and endearing feature of the 1500 cars was the famous light and responsive Alfa Romeo steering. The trait became virtually a hallmark of all future Alfa Romeos and the root of their hypnotic fascination for anybody who drives one. Obviously, any car that ran as many races of Targa Florio and Mille Miglia caliber as Alfa Romeo did *had* to have responsive steering and a quick, agile temperament. And if they were good in that kind of terrain they were no less than miraculous in normal driving.

If a 1.5-litre Alfa Romeo of such felicitous qualities was a good idea, an enlarged 1.75-litre version seemed an even better one. Vittorio Jano thought so too and in 1929 he substituted the slightly larger displacement cars over the full range of the old 1.5-litre models: the 6C 1750 *Turismo* of single-overhead-

The 2.3-litre "Monza" offered 60 mph in 6.9 seconds from rest and 120 mph, yet was a flexible and untemperamental sports car even in traffic.

ALFA ROMEO

cam design, the 6C 1750 *Gran Turismo* of double-overhead-cam construction, and the short-wheelbase 6C 1750 double-cam *Gran Sport*, sometimes supercharged. With this last car Jano seemed to have reached the inner circle, the very essence of a great sports car. The 6C 1750 *Gran Sport* represented an extraordinary balance: a chassis with irreproachable road manners and refreshing lack of temperament, and two-seater sports roadster coachwork with some of the most harmonious lines ever laid out on a coachbuilder's drawing board.

There have been other sports cars with style, speed, finesse, but not in quite the proportions in which they were arranged in the 6C 1750 Alfa Romeo, not with quite the balance of this car. The roadster body was the perfect complement of the chassis, and vice versa; and the magnificent sculpture under the hood merged science and art into one. A recent review of Luigi Barzini's latest book, *From Caesar to the Mafia*,* concluded with Barzini's treatment of "that very old tradition from which his countrymen cannot escape, most fortunately for us all—the innate necessity of putting beauty before practicality." In the 1750 Alfa Romeo, however, Jano went one step further and combined beauty and practicality in perfect proportions. And if there was any doubt that the scales were a little weighted toward beauty, one had no further to look than the Grand Prix races of Belgium, Spain, Rome, Tunis, and Monza, plus the Ulster Tourist Trophy, the Mille Miglia, and the Double Twelve race of Brooklands—all won in a single season by the civilized little 1750 Alfa Romeo!

In 1931 the model matured into the 8C 2300 with the addition of two cylinders (65 mm x 88 mm) to form a straight-eight

* Used with permission; *The Evening Sun,* Baltimore, Maryland; Helen F. Knipp.

The monoposto (single seater) P3 was a 2.6-litre Grand Prix car developed out of the "Monza" sports car. Until overwhelmed by the German teams of the middle 1930s it was an omnipotent Grand Prix car.

ALFA ROMEO

The celebrated 2.9-litre Alfa Romeo sports car.

ALFA ROMEO

of 2.3-litres with the virtues of the 1750 plus a bit more flexibility and effortlessness. A team of 2300s was prepared for the 1931 season and, after losing the Mille Miglia to Rudolf Caracciola's Mercedes-Benz SSK, went on to pick up where the 1750 had left off, adding the 1931 Targa Florio and the firm's first of four successive victories at Le Mans.

The 2.3-litre was genetically a sports car, having been logically developed from the 1.5-litre *Turismo*. Yet, as the record shows, the car could compete very successfully with full Grand Prix machinery—a distinction shared wtih some of the Bugattis, the SSK Mercedes-Benz, and very little else. Some of this success was undoubtedly due to the car's superb handling, probably even more because more of the world's top drivers steered Alfa Romeos. Almost all were Italian—melodious names like Luigi Arcangeli, Tazio Nuvolari, Antonio Ascari, Guiseppe Campari, Giulio Ramponi, Baconin Barzacchini. And there was one other, a fellow named Enzo Ferrari who formed the *Scuderia Ferrari* in 1929 to take over Alfa Romeo racing activity and later went on to do other things with automobiles. And there were some "foreigners" too: Lord Howe and Sir Henry Birkin who drove 2.3-litres, the Frenchmen Louis Chiron and Louis Wagner, and even Rudolf Carac-

The brilliant 8C 2900, the bare chassis, and the P3 Grand Prix car from which the sports model was directly derived.

ALFA ROMEO

ciola (Italian by ancestry but German by birth and residence) who was lured away from Stuttgart for the 1932 season. The Alfa Romeo drivers considered Caracciola enough of a "foreigner" to demand that his car not be red like the rest but white. Possibly they still smarted over his victory in the Mille Miglia last season with his SSK Mercedes-Benz, the first victory there for either a non-Italian car or a non-Italian driver. It was a feat which was repeated only once more, again by Mercedes in 1955 with an Englishman named Stirling Moss.

In order to give these drivers as much to work with as possible, Jano revised his masterwork again in 1932 to create the "Monza" which would give 60 mph in 6.9 seconds from rest and something on the order of 120 mph—not at all bad for a 2.3-litre even forty years later. Nevertheless, Alfa Romeo was doing battle against Grand Prix cars with basically sports cars and eventually the competition began to creep up. Something new was needed.

That something was the P3, the new Alfa Romeo *monoposto* or single-seater Grand Prix car which became one of the greatest GP cars of all time—*il ultimo Alfa.* As might be expected, the new P3 owed more than a little to the "Monza," with displacement up to 2.6 litres and a pair of superchargers, one for each block of four cylinders. The car was lightened as much as possible both with alloys and good design, and a dry weight of only 1700 pounds with 190 hp on demand promised an interesting return on the investment. And it was an investment which paid handsome dividends, a virtual Alfa Romeo monopoly of the race tracks of Europe. Grand Prix after Grand Prix fell to the red cars from Milano and what the P3 didn't take went, it seemed, to the 1750s and 2300s. The year 1932 was indisputably the year of the Alfa Romeo.

It is likely that the P3 would have gone on carrying all before it in the fashion of the P2 if the German government hadn't decided that international Grand Prix racing was an

The ultimate Alfa sports car, the 8C 2900 of 1937.

ALFA ROMEO

ideal propaganda media. The subsidies handed out to Mercedes-Benz and Auto-Union, although somewhat over-rated in later years, did give them an edge and permitted them to leapfrog conventional lines of development to produce fantastically advanced racing cars that eclipsed Alfa Romeo, Bugatti, Maserati, and everybody else.

However, it's an ill wind that blows nobody good and even being "stuck," as Alfa Romeo was, with a batch of obsolete Grand Prix cars and spare engines could have its benefits, particularly if you were a well heeled sports car buyer in 1937. While the P3 was outclassed as a Grand Prix car it most certainly was not as a sports car, and Jano proceeded to bore out the GP engines to 2.9 litres and de-tune them (also adding independent suspension to the chassis) to create the 8C 2900, which was easily the *ne plus ultima* Alfa Romeo of all time. Only 30 were offered for sale, in the area of $13,000 apiece, and among others who queued up to buy them were King Michael of Rumania and Prince Bernhard of the Netherlands, who hopefully guarded them as well as their crown jewels.

The 8C 2900 sports car was Alfa Romeo's highest contribution to the Golden Age. It marked the closing of an era for both Alfa Romeo and the world, yet the astute people at

A pair of interesting post-war bodies on the basically pre-war 6C 2500 chassis.

ALFA ROMEO

Milano had an almost uncanny sense of the feeling and philosophies which were to follow in the next epoch. The less esoteric 6C 2500 cars of 1939 and the advanced bodies which they later carried whispered of the great things which would again come from Italy when peace came. In those years the Alfa Romeo star might shine a little less brightly but no less proudly.

Chapter 9

MERCER AND THE RACEABOUT

The closest that most people come to a Mercer "Raceabout" is when they are handed a plastic model of one as a filling station promotional premium, or when they see one reproduced on Japanese-made beer steins or paper place mats. It is a pity that more people do not know more about one of the finest sports cars ever built in America, or that there are not more of them for people to know.

It is not difficult to see why the beer glass and souvenir plate makers frequently choose the silhouette of the Mercer "Raceabout" to adorn their wares. It is a striking and immediately interesting creation even to people who know little about cars. Everything was Spartan simplicity and purely functional; nothing was put on for "effect" and therein lies its great and enduring fascination.

Up front was a great brassbound honeycomb radiator with "Mercer" splashed across it in eight inch letters followed by a few feet of gleaming hood held in place by a stout leather strap. The hood ended abruptly in a slanting polished hardwood dashboard extending clear down to the low slung floorboard. Next came morocco-like leather seats backed by a great steel cylinder of fuel topped with a pair of no-nonsense-sized filler caps. There was hardly any coachwork to speak of save for a little rear mounted tool box and sturdy but wispy appearing fenders. Windshields were for maiden aunts, not Mercerites; although a glass "monocle" bolted onto the steering column was available as an extra. A massive brass shaft jutted up brusquely from the right hand side of the dash at nearly a forty-five-degree angle to thrust a man-sized wooden steering wheel directly into the driver's lap—no wonder Barney Oldfield drove underhand style! The brake lever mounted on the right side of the frame with the gearchange lever looked like a fugitive from a roundhouse repair shop. Brass headlamps, a big eye-catching brass searchlight mounted in the center of

The Mercer "Speedster" was the ancestor of the "Raceabout" and convinced the company that sports cars were the thing to build.
AUTOMOBILE MANUFACTURERS ASSOCIATION

the cowl, and brass acetylene-powered running lamps riding on each side are a joy forever to those who love the golden glow of polished brass and don't mind buying their Brasso, flannel cloths, and liniment in wholesale lots. The package was completed by a pair of spares bringing up the rear, road racing style. In total, it was—and is—something grand to behold.

The Mercer "Raceabout" had unique ancestry. While men like Marc Birkigt and W.O. Bentley gained their early experience and perspective in locomotive shops, and their cars sometimes showed it, the gentlemen behind the Mercer were bridge builders, with nothing less than the Brooklyn Bridge itself to their credit. The Roeblings were a rich and famous family of Trenton, New Jersey, with a touch for spectacular success in impressive undertakings. Early in the century they founded the "Mercer Automobile Company of Trenton, N.J." and hired an engineer named Planche to design a car for them. In 1907 their first-born, the "Roebling-Planche," appeared; a good quality but not extraordinary car. The first signs of greatness came two years later when the "Speedster" was offered for the first time. The influence of the popular Vanderbilt Cup races and lesser speed contests springing up around the country was apparently the *raison d'être* of the "Speedster" built for young men with nerve and $1950 who wanted to churn up the North Road in a cloud of yellow dust and imagine themselves at the head of the pack.

The Roeblings were convinced by the "Speedster" that sports cars were the things to build; not a particularly common viewpoint on this side of the Atlantic. So, they hired Finley Robertson Porter to design for them the best sports car that he could. Of course, nobody called sports cars "sports cars" in those days, so the product of Mr. Porter's inspired convictions of what an exciting car should be like was christened the Mercer "Raceabout"* and introduced to America in the untroubled year of 1910.

* It was only shortly before that the Roeblings' cars became known as Mercers, so called for Mercer County, New Jersey, where the Trenton plant stood.

The Roeblings were not disappointed with their new sports car and neither were their customers. Throughout nearly all of its five-year production span there was a waiting list for what was flamboyantly, but accurately, advertised as "The most talked about car in America." Its famous guarantee did not stress quality or reliability, although it had both in reasonable measure; it stressed *speed*. The Mercer Automobile Company of Trenton, N.J., guaranteed that the new "Raceabout" would show you a mile's worth of scenery in fifty-one seconds flat (just over 70 mph), and nowhere is it recorded that anybody asked for his money back.

The uncomplicated T-head engine designed by Finley Robertson Porter for the Mercer "Raceabout" was perhaps not quite what Porsche, Bugatti, and associates were up to at the time, but certainly no one could say that it didn't do its job—and then some. Porter's engine was a 306-cubic-inch four-cylinder, which works out to about one and a quarter litres per cylinder. It was a big, slow revving plant typical of the times and gave you its maximum of about 60 hp at under 2000 rpm. The torque was such that you could have top gear starts without fuss, although also without the crackling Mercer acceleration which came from going through the four speed gearbox. With the simplistic handling qualities of its stiff springing and low profile, comparatively light steering, top speed of about 80 mph, and its excellent visibility, the Mercer was an effective reply to Continental sports machinery. It seems a great pity that a proper Mercer team was not assigned to European duty in the days before World War I. The results might have been very interesting.

The "Raceabout" was lower, lighter, and more lithe appearing than its arch rival the Stutz "Bearcat," and aesthetically perhaps more pleasing to look upon. Often it was a dazzling vision of Mercer yellow striped in black, but you could also order a red car with black upholstery and trim, azure blue

A jaunty Mercer tourer with a lady driver, 1910.
AUTOMOBILE MANUFACTURERS ASSOCIATION

with white striping and black leather, a grey car with black, or a maroon body with black leather and gold striping. Whatever the color, any "Raceabout" had the same endearing schizophrenic personality, which would let you amble through town effortlessly enough not to ruffle milk wagon horses (provided the cut-out was not open) and then take you down a country road with a willingness that would run the fur off a jackrabbit. Perhaps not until the three-litre Bentley would there be a car which could be so simultaneously civilized in the city and savage on the open road.

Of course, as with all vamps, there was a price to be paid for pleasures received. The Mercer "Raceabout" had to be coaxed into co-operation with a routine that sounded like a countdown for a moon rocket. Among other things, before blasting off you got out and got into the motor: opening the cylinder priming cups and gassing them up to prime the engine, switching over to the correct half of the dual set of

Spartan simplicity; enduring appeal.

AUTHOR'S PHOTO

spark plugs, checking to be sure that there was sufficient pressure in the fuel system to keep gas flowing into the engine, and naturally spinning over the crank handle. It was not a car for Le Mans starts. In keeping the "Raceabout" as light as possible, Porter perhaps overdid it a bit in the frame which occasionally tended to sag if overly stressed, and the aluminum engine bearers could have been a little hardier. Stopping was at best a speculative proposition and required both the foot brake operating on the transmission and the hand brake which worked shoes on the rear wheels. Like the early Bugattis, Mercers were apparently intended to go rather than to stop. And since the car had no body to speak of, the driver and his passenger were completely at the mercy of the elements—but then wasn't that part of the fun? It is only in later years that sports car people have given up being Spartans and been converted to hedonism.

The "Raceabout" was naturally a young guy's ideal transport, but unfortunately he was the fellow who could usually least afford the $2600 that it took to own one. That was a great deal of money in the faraway days of the nickel beer and five cent cigar and fortunate was the fellow who had an understanding papa. The factory records indicate that under a thousand such gleeful young gentlemen were found. Nevertheless, the "Raceabout" was not like many of the ungrateful great cars which thanked their creators by driving them straight into a financial brick wall. It made money. The little plant in Trenton seldom turned out more than two or three "Raceabouts" a week, yet by 1915 the company was clearing an annual net profit of $125,000 or about 20% on its total investment. But then, the Mercer deserved to succeed. Didn't it typify all the old-fashioned Yankee virtues? Wasn't it a high quality, honestly built, enduring piece of merchandise from nameplate to tailpipe?

Part of the growing Mercer legend was forged on race courses from Savannah to Santa Monica in the rough and tumble of American road racing before World War I. The legend was nourished by the rivalry between Mercer and

A Mercer racer come to a sad end at Venice, California. The Mercer vs Stutz rivalry rose to fever pitch before World War I and was fought out on tracks all across the country.

SMITHSONIAN INSTITUTION

Stutz racing cars, as well as between the over-the-counter "Raceabout" and "Bearcat" models. The track battles came to a head in 1914 when Mercer fielded three cars for the Vanderbilt Cup race on February 26th at Santa Monica, California, to be driven by Spencer Wishart, Ed Pullen, and Barney Oldfield. Mercer had counted the great Ralph De Palma among its ranks but a feud between him and Oldfield caused De Palma to resign in a huff and enter the race on his own with his old faithful 1908 Grand Prix Mercedes. Pullen's Mercer took the lead shortly after the start and held it until he crashed about one third of the way through. The Wishart Mercer was soon out and the race evolved into a grudge match between Oldfield and De Palma at the head of the pack. All through the race De Palma had made not a single pit stop and on the 34th of 35 laps he signaled a stop for much needed tires on the next round. Oldfield, who was also riding on his last shreds of rubber, saw the signal and took his Mercer in for tires. But De Palma passed his own pits to gain time and sailed on to win the race scant seconds ahead of the yellow Mercer.

Two days after the Vanderbilt Cup race the American Grand Prize was to be run over the same 8.4-mile course at Santa Monica. Both Pullen and his Mercer had recovered from their crash in the Vanderbilt and joined the three other Mercers driven by Oldfield, Wishart, and Gordon—the last a private entry with a "Raceabout" engine. It was doubtful if De Palma could repeat his threat with his obsolescent car, and the Mercer-Stutz rivalry burned as brightly as ever. Almost from the beginning Mercer moved to dominance with Wishart in the lead and Oldfield close behind. But there was a long way to go—48 laps and over 400 miles—and Spencer Wishart's Mercer fell victim to too much too soon on the twenty-third lap. Now, Ed Pullen fought for glory, Mercer's and his own, as he fenced with Gil Anderson's Stutz and Barney Oldfield's Mercer. Then Oldfield dropped out with lubrication problems and it was Mercer vs Stutz fighting it out flat out, to the delight of a quarter of a million people. As the toe-to-toe endurance contest was waged through the California countryside, the Stutz began to waver and then gave up the ghost. The 1914 American Grand Prize was a glorious victory for car and driver. For Mercer, it was the first time that an American car had ever won the race; and for Pullen it was a Horatio Alger story come true for a through-the-ranks grease monkey who rose to the first rank of race drivers.

The road rivalries between the "Raceabout" and the "Bearcat" were less easily settled, especially without starters, measured courses, and defined finish lines. In fact, the battle between "Stutz nuts" and "worser Mercers" has raged for well over half a century, sometimes over dusty back roads but mostly in barber shops, beer gardens and pool halls. Recently, *Motor Trend* magazine decided to see how the two great

A piece of history frozen on film. Barney Oldfield relaxes at the wheel of his Mercer with trademark cigar and scans his press notices.

AUTOMOBILE MANUFACTURERS ASSOCIATION

American classic sports cars really did stack up against each other, perhaps for the last time that it would ever be done with the real hardware. A gentleman was found who owned one mint specimen of each—William Harrah of Reno, Nevada—and who was willing to let two of the most valuable cars in existence be road tested. Eric Dahlquist, *Motor Trend's* editor, was a bit cautious about flinging $150,000 worth of irreplaceable museum pieces over the Nevada desert, comparing the test to "talking the Smithsonian Institution out of the Wright Brothers glider for a day to relive the sensation at Kitty Hawk as perfectly as possible."

After spending a day with the ghosts of Barney Oldfield, Spencer Wishart, and perhaps Finley Robertson Porter and Harry C. Stutz hovering over his shoulder, Dahlquist confirmed what Mercer-ites have always known: that the Mercer

"Raceabout" was lower, lighter, and shorter; steered and handled better than its chief rival, could get away faster, and hold a slightly higher top speed. "On the dirt the Mercer will run rings around the Stutz flying through turns with the tail hung out, manufacturing an almost true sprint car attitude where the Stutz feels clumsy and heavy. . . . On the face of it the Mercer wins hands down."* On the other side of the scale, Dahlquist appreciated the Stutz's battery-operated coil which started the engine with a push button, and Harry Stutz's genuine transaxle which was years ahead of its time.

The Type 35 Mercer "Raceabout" passed into history in 1915, and much of the sparkle of the Mercer name went with it. The deaths of the Roebling brothers seemed to progressively gut the firm of its oldtime drive. Washington Roebling, the youngest brother, died along with 1516 other passengers

* Used with permission, *Motor Trend* magazine, Petersen Publishing Company, Los Angeles, California.

Spencer Wishart, a celebrated Mercer driver, poses at the wheel.
SMITHSONIAN INSTITUTION

on the *Titanic* in 1912, and F. W. and C. G. Roebling died in 1917 and 1918. A year later a Wall Street entrepreneur named E. S. Hare acquired control of the company and merged it with two other grand old names, Simplex and Locomobile.

A new "Raceabout" had appeared in 1915 under the Roeblings' regime to replace the original car. The wheelbase had been upped from 108 to 115 inches, the steering wheel was moved from right to left, the driver's seat set a bit further forward than the passenger's, and the wooden spoked artillery wheels gave way to wire. The elemental nakedness, too, was beginning to yield to the times. After the war the re-organized "Mercer Motors Company" picked up where the Roeblings had left off. The magic name "Raceabout" was still there but the blithe spirit was beginning to sag. Although the mile's worth of scenery was reduced from fifty-one to forty-eight seconds, the look of the post-war "Raceabout" was much less head-turning. It also became less dollar-turning. When Mercer revised its rather high priced four-cylinder Series 5 cars and announced the six-cylinder Series 6, a stodgy little "Runabout" with a rumble seat was catalogued at $3750. The "Raceabout" was gone forever, and after 1925 so was Mercer.

Chapter 10

THE ROYAL SPORTS CAR

Even in a golden age of great cars the Hispano-Suiza stood out like a Cellini among tinware. The "Hisso" meant different things to different people: a sports car, a luxury car, a flawless gem of the best auto engineering of the day, or—as the most expensive standard production car in history—a status symbol. In a sense, the Hispano-Suiza was the automotive counterpart of the Renaissance man. But it was not a case of being a talented dilettante at many things and master of none; whatever the Hispano did she did well. In that part of her life when she was primarily a sports car she quickly revolutionized *voiturette* or small car racing with a high efficiency, high speed multi-cylinder engine which pre-dated even Ettore Bugatti. As a grand lady of the twenties and thirties she was an aristocrat without peer. And as a femme fatale she conjured up what certainly must have been the most singularly exotic sports car of all time.

The Hispano-Suiza is further proof of the proposition that the really worthwhile things of art, architecture, and engineering have usually been the products of inspired *individual* minds. The mind in this case was that of Marc Birkigt, a Swiss-born engineer who graduated from the Geneva *Ecole des Arts et Métiers* in 1898 and began to look for prospects. The hunt took him to a most unlikely setting for the birth of one of the world's great cars, over the Pyrenees to Barcelona. There he went to work first as a designer of electric locomotives for a group of Spanish entrepreneurs. Both Birkigt and his employers were intrigued with the promise of the motorcar and the young Swiss was soon given the opportunity to try his hand. The result was the first automobile ever built in Spain. Soon a company was set up to manufacture Hispano-Suiza automobiles. The little firm had rough going in its early days, changing names and apparently capitalization three times in four years.

Both Birkigt and his backers persevered and while the financiers were getting the company on an even keel Birkigt progressed beyond his original two-cylinder model and developed a series of four-cylinder automobiles of increasing sophistication. By 1906 Hispano-Suiza was ready to exhibit at the great Paris show and offered a pair of four-cylinder cars with T-head engines. The following year Birkigt added a pair of sixes with "square" engines of equal bore and stroke, 115 x 115 mm and 130 x 130 mm.

People were beginning to notice Hispano-Suiza, and among them was Alphonso XIII, the young king of Spain. Along with most of European royalty and aristocracy Alphonso had been bitten by the automobile bug and it seemed that he developed a particularly severe case of "automania." He was, in his own language, an *aficionado* of the automobile and he enjoyed cars with a full blooded Latin passion. Since Birkigt's cars were the only Spanish natives a natural rapport grew up between Alphonso and Hispano-Suiza.

In 1909 Alphonso decreed that Spain would celebrate the automobile with a grand race. The king donated a trophy called the Catalan Cup, set up an eighteen-mile circuit on the outskirts of Barcelona, and invited entries from all over Europe. Naturally, Hispano-Suiza was expected to defend the national honor, and Birkigt responded with a team of racing voiturettes which were quite apart from most other designers' ideas about small racing cars. At that time a voiturette was not a scaled down version of a bigger racing car but an original one- or two-cylinder affair. In essence, what Birkigt did was to miniaturize his normal designs (and one of these ran to 10.3 litres) to produce a jewel-like 1.8-litre, four-cylinder car. A team of three of the new cars was prepared to run for the King's Catalan Cup, and the Spanish hopes rode with them.

King Alphonso XIII's race for the Catalan Cup run near Barcelona in 1909 launched Hispano-Suiza into a sports car program which led to the famous Type 15 T named in honor of the king. Here, Jules Goux in the winning Lion-Peugeot finishes ahead of the Hispano-Suiza.

AUTOMOBILES PEUGEOT

Those hopes rode high when Hispano-Suiza went to an early lead, but then a clutch problem and an accident eliminated two thirds of the team and the third car finished behind the French-entered Lion-Peugeot. However, since the other Lion-Peugeots, Sizare-Naudains, De Dion-Boutons and other French cars had all fallen by the wayside along the 227.5 miles, second place was no disgrace for Hispano-Suiza's maiden race.

The 1910 Hispano-Suiza racing voiturette had a bore and stroke of 65 x 140 mm, and for 1911 Birkigt extended the stroke to 200 mm to give him 2.6 litres, plus making a few other changes such as going to wire wheels. With this car Birkigt planned to work revenge on the French, who had bested him again on home ground for the 1910 Catalan Cup. Hispano-Suiza entered the 1910 *Coupe des Voiturettes* to be run at Boulogne. The extra year of development vindicated Birkigt's ideas about the four-cylinder voiturette when a Hispano-Suiza beat the nearest French competitor by over a quarter of an hour to win the *Coupe des Voiturettes*. Birkigt had planted a milestone in the development of the sports car and made the old single/double-cylinder cars obsolete overnight. It was a moment of pride for Birkigt and for a king whose country, for the most part, still languished in the eighteenth century.

The victorious racing car was an excellent point of departure for a commercial version, and Birkigt saw the opportunity. He increased the displacement again to 3.6 litres—still very modest by contemporary measure—to give greater flexibility to the engine and the new model was catalogued at the "Type 15 T." Naturally, King Alphonso tried one of the early cars and was enormously pleased with its verve, easy handling, and top speed of about 85 mph. The fact that it was easy on fuel and fairly cheap to buy at $2000 chassis price

The Type 15 T or "Alphonso XIII" Hispano-Suiza, named for the King of Spain, was among the earliest true sports cars.
BRIGGS CUNNINGHAM AUTOMOTIVE MUSEUM

"In proud flight over the head of scores of phantom horses" . . . *Le Cigogne Volante.*

AUTHOR'S PHOTO

The idol of an age. When Marc Birkigt's 6.5-litre, single-overhead-cam, six-cylinder car was introduced at the Paris Salon of 1919 it created a sensation as the most advanced—and most expensive—car in the world.

COLLECTION OF M. L. BUD COHN

did not concern him, although it did interest conventional buyers quite a bit. Alphonso buzzed the boulevards of Barcelona in the Type 15 T and pounded it over the rough country roads until he was satisfied enough to let Birkigt name the car for him, the Alphonso XIII Hispano-Suiza. Down through the years it has remained a singular honor: the only royal sports car.

After a while Birkigt began to look for ways to improve the Type 15 T, apparently for the forthcoming 1912 *Coupe de l'Auto*, and he came up with an interesting scheme to supercharge the car. The basic concept was not new; Gottlieb Daimler had experimented with force-fed engines well before the turn of the century, and the American Chadwick is generally claimed to be the first successful supercharged car. But the extraordinary way that Birkigt went about supercharging the 15 T was purely his own. Instead of a "blower," Birkigt added two extra cylinders to the normal four-cylinder engine which were unfired. Working as air pumps, these two dummy cylinders fed air under pressure to the other four cylinders. On the return stroke they helped to suck out the exhaust gases. It sounded like a practical system but it wasn't ready in time for the 1912 race and after that Birkigt seems to have lost interest in the idea.

By 1914 Hispano-Suiza was offering a fairly elaborate line of cars ranging from a little 12 hp car to a powerful 75 hp six-cylinder car, but the Alphonso was far and away the most famous and best seller. Since its introduction in 1910, the Type 15 T's suspension had been improved and the three-speed box had been replaced with a four. But with the coming of the war the Birkigt talents were diverted to the design of aircraft engines, and cars were temporarily put aside. He quickly produced a V-8 aero engine of lightweight alloy construction that became one of his most famous successes. It was officially adopted by the French government and Birkigt came to Bois Columbes near Paris to set up a factory, less than four miles from where Bugatti was working at Pateaux. The same American mission that adopted Bugatti's sixteen-cylinder aero engine also chose the Hispano V-8 for production in America and many of the American "Jennys" were powered by Hispano-Suiza engines built here under license. The light and highly efficient engine (300 hp, later increased to 375 hp) was built in four countries and about 50,000 were completed before the Armistice.

While World War I swept away a grand era for most people and many institutions, it began a new and glittering one for Marc Birkigt and Hispano-Suiza. Despite the disruption to his automotive plans and the long hours of fatiguing work, the war was a rather fortuitous and timely event for Birkigt. The experiments with lightweight alloys and experience with increasing power output taught valuable lessons which would have taken years longer to learn, and profitable licensing agreements gave Hispano-Suiza the money to put it all into practice when peace came. Birkigt had never been so enthused with racing as Bugatti, the Duesenbergs and others—perhaps it went against his practical Swiss nature—and now he seemingly abandoned the sports car in favor of the most advanced super luxury car the world had yet seen.

The car came soon, less than a year after the Armistice, and when it was shown at the Paris Salon in 1919 it was so brilliantly conceived, so far ahead of its time, and so beautifully executed that it created a sensation. Birkigt had succeeded in combining the best of everything in just-right proportions to create a car which was, by the standards of 1919 and for a good while thereafter, virtually flawless. At the heart of the matter was a 6.5-litre, six-cylinder engine of single-overhead-cam design which had been derived from one bank of a V-12 air engine that had not gotten into production by the end of the war. The new automobile engine was a summation of Birkigt's wartime experience with alloys and every possible part of it was of alloy construction, with nitralloy steel liners screwed into the lightweight block. The devotion to absolute quality was total, and quite unduplicable by the standards of the 1970s. For example, the overhead camshaft, which rode in seven main bearings, was a true work of metal crafters' art. It started out as nearly eight hundred pounds of the finest steel that money could buy and finished as a hundred pounds of hand polished perfection.

It is said that when Niccolo Machiavelli sat down to write he put on his best clothes to honor the occasion. Birkigt similarly felt that when his great engine was at work it should also look its best, and to assure that it did he was willing to go to considerable effort. The head was finished in a black vitreous enamel that was pressure-applied with a secret process and which seems to have remained impervious to almost anything, including the passage of half a century. The name "Hispano-Suiza" in bright letters stood out from the great monolith of black, and the rest of the engine compartment was a majestic assemblage of hand polished alloy parts, with probably more man hours invested in its beauty alone than it takes to build a dozen Mustangs. From the base of the engine polished alloy pans flared out to shield all this underhood elegance from the indignity of road splash. Of course, the beauty under the bonnet didn't make the Hisso run one bit better but it gave the car an enduring integrity which will almost surely never again be matched.

The Hispano frame was a massive ladder of chrome steel fitted front and rear with half elliptic springs of conventional design but with some mysterious qualities all their own. They gave the car very fine roadholding ability, plus an inexplicable smoothness. David Scott-Moncrieff, who had probably owned and driven more great cars than anyone else alive, claims that the Hispano had "a capacity for ironing out lumps and pot holes" which he thought was only possible in cars with independent suspension.

Since Birkigt intended his car as a luxury carriage which would probably do most of its service whisking aging millionaires and diamond studded dowagers at sedate speeds along the Champs Elysée, there is no reason why he should have paid more than normal attention to its brakes. But he did. Although it would be the middle of the decade before many other passenger cars got four-wheel brakes Birkigt had brakes at each corner of his car in 1919, but he went further than that. Hisso wheels had huge finned aluminum drums, and the brakes were power operated by means of a servo mechanism operating off the gearbox. Without doubt, the Hispano-Suiza stopped better than any other car on the road. So well, in fact, that the system confounded even Sir Henry Royce who abandoned his own ideas about four-wheel brakes and adopted the Hispano-Suiza system under license. Rolls-Royce, Ltd liked it so well that, with modifications, the system was used on Rolls-Royce cars until the advent of disc brakes on the 1966 Silver Shadow.

Up to now the Hispano-Suiza emblem had been a handsome winged radiator badge incorporating–naturally–Swiss and Spanish symbology. But with the coming of the new car it was felt that something a little more grand was called for; something on the order of Charles Sykes' "Spirit of Ecstasy" which graced the Rolls-Royce radiator cap. Hispano-Suiza had no further to look than its own history for the perfect symbol. During the World War I dogfights, squadrons of French Spads with Hispano engines blasted their way to glory in the skies over France, and none of them basked in more raw glamour than Captain Georges Guynemer's *Escadrille des Cigognes Volantes,* the Flying Storks. The graceful, big winged birds of the Alsace chimney pots seemed the perfect emblem of effortless flight. So, Birkigt commissioned a famous French sculptor, René Bazin, to capture the spirit of *Le Cigogne Volante* and to put it "in proud flight over the head of scores of phantom horses," as Michael Arlen the novelist described the Hispano mascot in *The Green Hat.* The wingtips, in a downward stroke, were attached to the radiator cap in such a way that the little statue really appeared to be flying unattached to the car. Like the rest of the car it was done to

Hispano-Suiza super sports car, the celebrated "Boulogne" with an aluminum "boat tail" body by Kellner of Paris. Car is powered with a six-cylinder, eight-litre, SOHC engine with a high-lift cam.
BRIGGS CUNNINGHAM AUTOMOTIVE MUSEUM

jewel-like perfection and then silverplated, and owners were advised to avoid "the usual abrasives" and treat it with the respect due old Sheffield.

Birkigt happily avoided the Duesenberg brothers' misfortune with their first passenger car, the Model A, which was a mechanical gem but a car without the style to match its technical sophistication. In addition to the quality of its "hardware," the Hispano-Suiza had enormous cachet, and in an amazingly short time established itself as "the" car to own. Adopted and adored by the 1920's equivalent of the jet set, ownership of a Hisso became *de rigeur* and one was socially safe in a Hispano from the Promenade des Anglais to Sunset Boulevard. The world's highest priced chassis at $11,000 added to the esoteric image, and a complete car with lush bodywork could run to $20,000 or more. Hollywood of the twenties took the Hispano to its heart and *Le Cigogne Volante* frolicked happily in the California sunshine. Perhaps the one that flew the highest was Rudolf Valentino's magnificent convertible coupe which reportedly cost $25,000. Certainly the oddest belonged to a gentleman who "Indianized" it. Over the flawless lacquer he had a circle of Indian symbols painted on, the seats upholstered with Navajo blanketing, and on the back it wore an enormous Indian basket as a luggage carrier.

The 6.5-litre Hispano did not offer considerably more than 80–85 mph, mainly because it was conceived to give maximum performance and pleasure at normal touring speeds and was, supposedly, not a sporting car. However, its superior road manners and braking coupled with the delivery of quick power with the solid assurance of a locomotive suggested that the car was good for something more than conventional limousine duty. Rich Hispanophiles astutely sensed this and began asking Birkigt for a hot Hispano. Chief among them was André Dubonnet, heir to the liqueur fortune and amateur race driver of considerable talent. Birkigt was reluctant, but yielded a bit in 1922 and offered a car with its wheelbase shortened from the standard 145¼ inches to 133¼ inches and top speed above 90 mph. The factory—now operating primarily from Bois Columbes in France—was not particularly disposed to racing and the first sporting Hispano since the Alphonso XIII was raced privately in Italy in 1922 and accounted itself well enough to be called the "Monza." The next year brought an even hotter Hispano when Birkigt enlarged the 6.5-litre engine to 8 litres, bringing horsepower to 144 at 2500 rpm. When this 100 mph plus car won the Georges Boillot Cup at Boulogne in 1923, taking second place and fastest lap time as well, it became known as the Boulogne Hispano and began a legend.

The Boulogne was a rare car; only fifteen were made in all but they wove a scarlet thread through the fabric of a golden age. And by far the most scarlet of the lot was a very special sports roadster built for that patron saint of Hispanos, André Dubonnet. Dubonnet had driven Boulognes in the 1923 racing season, which included a 1-2-3 Hispano victory at San Sebastian, Spain, that year. For 1924 he entertained visions of attacking the Targa Florio, for which even he had to admit that the Hispano was not the most eminently suited car. But Latin passion is not easily denied and Dubonnet ordered a new Boulogne with the high-lift-cam racing engine. When he took delivery of the chassis, Dubonnet had his own mechanics lower the profile by changing to flatter springs and cutting down the radiator. Then he sent the amended chassis to Nieuport Aviation which clothed it with what must certainly rank as the most unique body ever put on a car. First, a super-thin alloy skin was stretched over a lightweight frame and then covered with strips of tulipwood which were attached to the metal shell with rivets. The result was the lightest and most flexible body possible for a car of the Hispano's size—and a piece of exotica worthy of Nebuchadnezzar. Despite six tires sacrificed to the Sicilian mountains, Dubonnet managed to finish sixth, and even more important he did not wreck the most exotic of an exotic breed.

The aperitif king was not alone in his almost blind devotion to the Boulogne. Charles T. Weymann, the creator of the lightweight Weymann patent "fabric" bodies, was also a His-

SAFETY STUTZ

pano disciple. Late in 1927 he found himself in a London nightclub in the company of some other gentlemen of the auto industry who were locked in heated debate over the merits of European versus American cars. Among them was Fred Moskovics, the president of Stutz. Confidence mounted on each side as the evening dwindled and when the group hit the damp English air outside both camps probably had some misgivings about Moskovics and Weymann wagering $25,000 on the outcome of a match race between Hispano and Stutz over the bricks of Indianapolis Motor Speedway for a full twenty-four hours.

The public, however, loved the idea. The bout of the century—the cream of the Continent in a fist fight with the boy next door for big money and all in their own back yard. Both sides were confident and each had a logical argument to back up his viewpoint. Stutz had virtually the only car in the country which could hope to match the Hispano (the "J" Duesenberg was still months away). Moskovics relied on its low profile, underslung chassis for quick cornering and on the proven durability of his high-revving engine for endurance—it had never failed in a single race. The Hisso had a three-litre edge—8 litres to the Stutz's 4.9—superior acceleration, and the special high-lift cam as used in Dubonnet's Targa Florio car. The only people seemingly opposed were the dealers of each marque, who saw disaster if their side lost; and very probably Marc Birkigt who still didn't think of his car as a sports machine at all. Weymann was, of course, strictly on his own with no formal factory backing while Moskovics had the whole Stutz factory a few minutes away from the Speedway.

The affair was properly carried off; no back road spectacle for a fence rail audience, this. Both sides met on the appointed

Stutz Vertical Eight vanquished by Charles Weymann's Hispano-Suiza at Indianapolis Motor Speedway in the match race of the decade in April 1928.

INDIANAPOLIS MOTOR SPEEDWAY CORP.

field of combat with the amenities of a dueling party under the Oaks in old New Orleans. At 1:00 o'clock sharp one Hispano-Suiza Boulogne and one BB Blackhawk Stutz stood side by side, ready. Then the starter gave the signal and they were away. The Hisso's superior acceleration gave it an immediate lead. This startled the Stutz driver, Tom Rooney, and apparently saw even more performance from the Hispano than he had been led to expect. Stutz strategy had been to pace the car until late in the race, hoping that the Hispano would pall under the twenty-four-hour grind, and then to press hard in the last laps. But now Rooney threw strategy to the winds and kicked his spurs into the Stutz. It was a victory of emotion over logic, and a costly one for Stutz. When Rooney

The last of the line, the great Type 68 with the 11.3-litre engine, as a dual cowl sports phaeton by Henri Binder of Paris.

BRIGGS CUNNINGHAM AUTOMOTIVE MUSEUM

blew his cool he also blew a valve tappet lock nut, and despite frequent ministrations by the pit crew there was little to be done and the Stutz retired about 8:00 o'clock the following morning while the Hispano was still going strong and miles ahead. Moskovics conceded defeat to Weymann—now $25,000 to the good for his faith in Hispano—but asked if Weymann had any objection to finishing the race against a fresh Stutz, just to see what would happen. Weymann agreed and the race continued.

This time a different story unfolded. Stutz's strategy was rigidly followed in the remaining three and a half hours and the Stutz finished with a seven-mile lead. Of course, the press and history have recorded the match race as a Hispano victory, but not without a lot of controversy over which was really the best car. In retrospect, it was perhaps at best a contest with blurred edges: a sports car that often masqueraded as a luxury car—Stutz—running against a luxury car revised as a sports car.

In 1931 Hispano-Suiza lost an old friend and gained a new model. The friend was Alphonso who hastily abdicated his throne, reportedly making a quick retreat from his court in a French-bodied Duesenberg and leaving behind a royal garage of about thirty of the finest cars on earth, a good percentage of them Hispano-Suizas. The happier of the two events of that unhappy year was the coming of the Type 68 Hispano-Suiza, one of the most imposing and ambitious cars of all time. Throughout the twenties the market *de grand luxe* had been pretty thoroughly conquered by the 6.5 and eight-litre, six-cylinder Hispanos. However, Birkigt felt that the new decade of the thirties called for a new standard in power, prestige and elegance. And, again ahead of his time, Birkigt provided it.

The new car drew upon Birkigt's vast experience with vee-type aero engines and was a V-12 of 9.4 litres which delivered a seemingly bottomless supply of power with both silky smoothness and sporting verve. Although the new Hisso did not come quite as a bolt out of the blue the way the six-

1928 "convertible victoria" on the Hispano-Suiza H6B chassis, coachwork by Henri Chapron of Paris.

AUTHOR'S PHOTO

cylinder had back in 1919—the rest of the world having caught up a bit—it was the epitome of the ultra refined automobile. In philosophy, the V-12 was simply a logical extension of the six with twice as many cylinders (and spark plugs; 24 with its dual ignition system), over 100 more horsepower, and the same incredible devotion to quality. To demonstrate that quality the Hispano people had Charles Faroux, the French motoring writer and past president of the ACF, drive one of the new V-12s from Paris to Nice and back as fast as he could. When the father figure of French motoring arrived back in Paris he drove the car into the Hispano showrooms onto a sheet of white paper and everyone waited for the first drop of oil to fall from the engine. It never did.

The six-cylinder cars had had their enlarged eight-litre Boulogne and in 1934 the twelves got their big brother, the incredible, almost legendary, 11.3-litre Type 68. Now there was some 250 hp delivered from the big engine turning at a very leisurely 3000 rpm and acceleration was on the order of 0 to 50 mph in 9.4 seconds with a car which seldom weighed less than 5000 pounds and carried every possible luxury. Of course, the chassis, suspension, steering, and brakes were quite capable of dealing with all this, but Birkigt still did not think of the Type 68 as a sports car. Perhaps not, but if it wasn't a sports car the Type 68 Hispano-Suiza on the short or légere chassis* was certainly the grandest Grand Touring car the world is ever likely to see.

* Four chassis types were available: short—11 feet 3 inches; légere (light)—12 feet 2 inches; normal—12 feet 6 inches; long—13 feet 2 inches. Chassis price for the Type 68 was $13,750, again the most expensive standard production chassis in the world.

Chapter 11

THE GREAT WHITE MERCEDES

When April came to the pretty Rhone countryside outside Lyons in 1914 it brought with it a group of visitors from Stuttgart with seven rough-looking automobiles. The little village hotel where they put up was glad for the trade; there were tensions and rumors of war with the Germans but business was business. But if only that German racing team manager didn't have to blow that whistle every morning at 5:00 A.M. to assemble his drivers. Day after day the whistle blew at five sharp and the seven drivers turned out and marched down to their cars to take them around the 23.3-mile course laid out by the Auto Club de France for its forthcoming Grand Prix in July.

Never in the history of motor sport had a racing team analyzed its field of combat so thoroughly, or for so long. Usually, when a car manufacturer went racing he simply built the best car he could, hired the best drivers he could, and tried to see that they got in some practice laps so at least they would know where they were going on race day. They didn't always know that much; in the 1904 Gordon Bennett race the

French driver Jules Salleron asked the stewards for a map of the course shortly before the start! In contrast, these people from Stuttgart wanted to know considerably more than where they were going. They wanted to know each hill, bend and curve in the course with unfailing memory, how fast they could take it, and in which gear. No detail was too small to be noted, analyzed and considered.

After a few weeks the drivers, mechanics and team manager apparently had all they needed to know and one morning the whistle didn't blow. For about a month the hotel s guests slept later and then one morning there was a shrill blast at 5:00 A.M. followed by the clumping of feet down the stairs. The drivers and their leader were the same but their cars had changed. They were a little less homemade looking now, and a bit shorter. Less visibly, their gear ratios had changed too. More testing. Then back to Germany, and back again to Lyons. To a serious observer, it was obvious what was going on: the Mercedes cars were being tailored to the course until they fit it like a glove.

Curiously, the French paid little attention to all this coming and going and they certainly weren't intimidated by it. Two years before, Peugeot had obtained the services of the young Swiss engineer Ernest Henri to design a new high performance car for them. With a single stroke Henri forecast the future of high performance cars for decades to come with his double-overhead-camshaft, four-valves-per-cylinder engine. With this very fine car and their superstar of racing, Georges Boillot, the French collected victories and records by the champagne bucketful in 1912 and 1913, including the first of three wins at Indianapolis. Their confidence for the 1914 race at Lyons was well founded. Part of the gala mid-summer Mardi Gras before the race was, for the French, merely a head start on the victory celebration.

In the years after they won the French Grand Prix in 1908, Mercedes' interest in racing diminished as they devoted more energies to developing new aero engines. The pursuits merged in the 1913 French Grand Prix when Mercedes ran cars carrying slightly modified aero engines, with quite modest success. At least they found out that what worked well to produce fairly constant engine speeds for flight was not so suitable for automotive use where engine speeds run up and down the rev range much more frequently. But Paul Daimler and his engineers at Stuttgart felt that their air engine techniques could be successfully adapted to automobiles. So, when *Daimler Motoren Gesellschaft* decided to make an appearance at Lyons in 1914 they followed their own line of thought for the new 4.5-litre formula rather than copying Henri as everyone else seemed to be doing. The result of this decision was an epic

The 1914 Grand Prix Mercedes at speed in the French Grand Prix at Lyons. This car successfully adapted advanced aero engine techniques to competition cars and greatly influenced sports car design in the years following World War I.

DAIMLER-BENZ A.G.

Short chassis Targa Florio type 28/95 Mercedes. With this basically pre-war car Mercedes re-entered sports car racing in 1921, with Max Sailer's history making drive from Stuttgart to Sicily to run in the Coppa Florio. In 1922 this model was supercharged and continued in use as a successful sports car up to the time of the "S" series.

THE BRIGGS CUNNINGHAM AUTOMOTIVE MUSEUM

and very influential car, plus one of the most important automobile races ever run.

Daimler disdained Henri's twin-cam arrangement and used a single-overhead cam to activate his four, 60-degree-inclined valves per cylinder, with three spark plugs in each combustion chamber. With its pressure lubrication system the car could sustain a high 3200 rpm for extended periods to take advantage of its full 115 hp. If Daimler's engine was different from Henri's on top it was even more so below. Henri used an ordinary cast iron block, while Daimler adapted the more costly and complex individually welded up water jacket system used in his air engines, which was not only lighter and stronger but provided superior cooling. The chassis was basically conventional, except for the Mercedes coil spring rebound dampers, and had only two-wheel brakes against the

PNEUS PIRELLI
PIRELLI
TRAGUARDO
VIIa TARGA FLORIO
29 MAGGIO 1921
PIRELLI
28

Peugeot's four-wheel stopping system. The chassis dropped low, fully a foot under the massive, Wagnerian 1908 GP car, and the rakish vee radiator and crisp lines put the car in a class with the Type 35 Bugatti as one of the most beautiful Grand Prix cars ever built. An English reporter at Lyons seemed more impressed with the Mercedes' looks than with the Peugeot's promised performance, writing that the Mercedes cars "have lines which a camera cannot portray; a white marble model of one would be a priceless possession."

In sum, the Mercedes was a very well thought out car which combined Daimler's newly learned lessons on aero engines with high-performance automotive practice. As the months before July 4th and the Grand Prix passed and the team shuttled back and forth between Stuttgart and Lyons, the new Mercedes was honed into a fine edged sword.

Daimlers' plans for wielding this weapon went further than measuring gradients and changing gear ratios to match the Lyons course: they involved a very definite, carefully planned strategy which was not only aware of Peugeot's strength but also traded on it. For the first time in racing a contest had been plotted like a military campaign with strategic maneuvers and alternate moves. The Mercedes strategy centered as much on Georges Boillot himself as on his car. Boillot was a grandstander who played to the crowds like a Booth or Barrymore of auto racing, and there was his Achilles heel. This time he was backed only by Jules Goux in the other Peugeot, while Mercedes had entered the limit of five cars, driven by Christian Lautenschlager, Max Sailer, Louis Wagner (a Frenchman), Otto Salzer and Theodore Pilette. Simply, the plan was for Sailer to harry Boillot from the start of the race and to capitalize on his need to be number one, and for this task Sailer's number 14 Mercedes was considered expendable. In the first lap Wagner beat Boillot by eighteen seconds, the French crowds gasped amazement, and Boillot took the bait.

The Targa Florio, 1921; scene of Max Sailer's glory with the 28/95 Mercedes.

Both drivers pushed their cars and themselves for all they were worth and the next few laps contained some very fine motor sport. On the sixth lap Sailer's Mercedes gave up and French confidence returned as the German threat seemed to pass.

In the Mercedes pits expressions were stoic as the second phase of the plan went into operation. Now Lautenschlager unobtrusively moved up behind Boillot with Salzer and Wagner supporting him from behind. Pilette stayed in the background as reserve to be called up if something happened to one of the other white cars. As the laps peeled off, the three Mercedes worked their way up to cut Boillot off from the rest of the pack and the battle settled down to a match between Gallic passion and German logic.

In the stands and all around the course spectators were being treated to one of the great races of all time. On the curves, such as *Les Descents des Esses* in full view of the stands, the Peugeots with their four-wheel brakes held an advantage, but on the straights the incredible acceleration of the Mercedes took over, and the balance see-sawed back and forth dramatically.

With only three rounds out of twenty left to go Boillot still held onto his lead by a thin twenty-three seconds. The next time around Lautenschlager made his move and passed Boillot, whose blue car was now surrounded by German racing white. On the next to last lap Boillot drove with all the skill and passion he could summon, but Lautenschlager's lead continued to increase. The pace finally caught up with the flogged Peugeot in the final lap and it simply gave up and never made it back to the finish line. In a triumph of careful technical development, team strategy, and measured driving Mercedes earned a resounding 1-2-3 victory.

The shock of the Mercedes sweep at the 1914 French Grand Prix was seismic, especially when France found itself facing the same kind of strength in the skies a few weeks later. And it was a shock which carried over the war years to post-war sports cars virtually undiminished. Even after nearly four years of devastating warfare the English respect for the German Mercedes had not lessened. Three months before the Armistice a leading English motor journal was campaigning for "a genuine British car built on Mercedes lines . . . which would make a prime favourite after the war." And of course that was exactly what one Englishman named Walter Owen Bentley had in mind. Bentley and a lot of other people who started to build sports cars after World War I looked closely at the GP Mercedes and not the least of them were the people at Daimler's.

The pre-war experiments with aero engines which had spawned the great GP car also gave birth to a lively sporting car, what the Germans called a *Hoechsleistung Tourenwagen*, or high performance touring car. These were big 7.2-litre, six-cylinder, overhead-cam cars—handsome, formidable looking machines which gave just a hint of what was to come from Stuttgart at the height of the golden age. The 28/95, as the model was known, was continued in production immediately after the war and soon a short wheelbase sports model ap-

One of the most coveted of all the great cars, an SSK Mercedes-Benz which represented the zenith of Dr. Ferdinand Porsche's stay at Stuttgart in the 1920s.

DAIMLER-BENZ A.G.

peared. With this car and the 1914 GP model—now fitted with front-wheel brakes—Mercedes launched itself back onto the racing scene, and with amazing promptness considering the chaos in post-war Germany. The first big success came when Max Sailer drove from Stuttgart to Sicily in a 28/95 sports car to compete in the Coppa and Targa Florio events. Simply for a citizen of vanquished Germany to make the drive presented legal and political problems, not to mention the practical ones of sufficient supplies of black market gas, oil and tires. But Sailer not only got the car to the starting line on schedule, he got it over the finish line to win first place in the Coppa Florio and second place in the Targa Florio (racing car category).

The Italians were to see more of the proud, vee-nosed German cars hurrying through the Sicilian mountains. Next year they arrived in force with the Italian Count Masetti at the head of the column driving his own personal 1914 GP Mercedes, followed by Lautenschlager and Salzer in 28/95s which now sounded more ferocious than ever, and a mysterious little pair of 1.5-litre cars called the 6/25/40 that moved very quickly. Count Masetti waged a great battle with a pair of French Ballots to win the Targa Florio that year, and the other Mercedes cars took more than enough awards to convince any doubters that Daimler's was very much back in the sports car business.

The high pitched wail of the 28/95s and the still higher screams of the little 6/25/40s echoing in the Sicilian mountains signaled a new era for Mercedes sports and racing cars—the era of the supercharger. While DMG was building WW I aero engines it found that planes suffered from engine starvation at high altitude. So, Paul Daimler harked back to some of

Long louvered hood, sweeping fendersnickle, plated external exhausts flowing from a big supercharged, overhead-cam engine: the very essence of the Golden Age. Mercedes-Benz "S" type four-seater of 1927 is owned by M. L. Post, President of Le Cercle Concours d'Elegance.

COURTESY M. L. BUD COHN

his father's experiments of the 1880s on the force feeding of engines and came up with a practical supercharging system to cram more air and fuel into the cylinders. After the war he lost no time adapting the experience to automobiles. In 1919 he tried the system first on a small sleeve-valve car and soon applied it to the 28/95 sports, and by 1921 he had two supercharged sports models on exhibit at the Berlin motor show. It was the smaller of these which ran in Sicily in 1922. Other people had supercharged cars before, the American Chadwick before World War I and Marc Birkigt's experimental Alphonso XIII for example, and other people would soon follow Mercedes' success and build blown cars. But no one else did it quite like Daimler. While other systems sucked the air-gas mixture out of the carburetor, the Mercedes blower forced the air under pressure *into* the carburetor. The main difference was that it made the car scream like something supernatural when the accelerator was depressed all the way to cut in the blower on demand. As Daimler's developed the supercharged sports car through the twenties, the howling white cars at speed became the symbol of an age.

Paul Daimler had started Mercedes down the road to future glory in a supercharged sports car and in 1923 the great Austrian auto engineer Ferdinand Porsche took over the wheel and shifted up to high gear. After attending to an un-cooperative two-litre supercharged GP car and some other duties Porsche took up the matter of a replacement for the aging 28/95, but he still remained faithful to the Daimler concept of the *Hoechsleistung Tourenwagen*. Initially, there were two supercharged cars, a four-litre and a six-litre, and both were robust, comfortable cars capable of moving well. Although they seemed to lean a little more toward touring than sporting, the six-litre apparently carried on the competition tradition well enough, Daimler-Benz reporting that the car "figured no

SS Mercedes-Benz "Super Sport" with owner Bud Cohn at the wheel. Car has the enlarged 7.1-litre engine and is believed to hold a record for the number of Concours prizes won.

COLLECTION OF M. L. BUD COHN

fewer than thirty-seven times in the list of successes for 1925."

Since both Porsche and the four- and six-litre cars were both newcomers to Stuttgart in 1923 it is possible, even likely, that at least the groundwork for the cars was laid before Porsche left Weiner-Neustadt in Austria. If the two cars, known properly as the 15/70/100 and the 24/100/140 (taxable hp/actual hp/hp with supercharger engaged), were a merger of Paul Daimler and Ferdinand Porsche concepts then it is simply another example of the amazing continuity and smooth transfer of power which had always seemed to characterize Daimler's. While other outstanding cars of the golden age generally bore the imprint of one man, such as Bugatti, Royce, Birkigt, Duesenberg and Bentley, Mercedes cars went through a succession of designers—Gottlieb Daimler, Wilhelm Maybach, Paul Daimler, Ferdinand Porsche, Hans Nibel, Max Sailer—and yet they

An especially gaunt 1927 Mercedes-Benz "S" type owned by Mr. Peter Ustinov and presently on loan to the Montagu Motor Museum.

MONTAGU MOTOR MUSEUM

370 S "Manheim" sports Mercedes-Benz of 1931 had something of the appearance of its bigger brothers, the S, SS, and SSK sports cars, but a smaller three-litre engine. Despite its lesser performance the 370 S survives as a beautifully balanced example of the classic sports car.

COLLECTION OF M. L. BUD COHN

Mercedes-Benz 170 sports roadster of 1934, a four-cylinder 1.7-litre car of moderate performance but excellent suspension and rakish lines.

COLLECTION OF M. L. BUD COHN

Sporting verve with a formal touch, 1936 500 K Mercedes-Benz with custom body by the English coachbuilder Corsica.

OWNER: JACK MILLER

have always been, and still are, unmistakably Mercedes. Anyway, in 1926 it was Ferdinand Porsche alone who started the process which was to transform a good car into a great one.

In that year Porsche revised the 24/100/140 by slightly increasing the displacement to 6.25-litres and in return got 110 hp at 2800 rpm in normal running or 160 hp with the supercharger engaged. The original long-wheelbase car was kept in the catalogue, but Porsche chopped down the original 12.3-foot-wheelbase to 11.2 feet to create a new sportier version which gave the type its enduring name—"K" for *kurz* or short. The year of the "K," 1926, was also the year in which Daimler and Benz merged to form *Daimler-Benz Aktiengesellschaft*, and from that time on built Mercedes-Benz automobiles. Porsche's new "K" proved to be a good omen for the new company. Despite the price—about $8000 for the chassis—people took to the "K" in good numbers and some very beautiful custom bodies were created for it, especially the sports phaetons. Daimler-Benz A.G. seemed particularly proud of its first-born, claiming that "this car enjoyed the reputation at the time of being the fastest touring car in existence, and coupled with its other qualities of road holding, ability to maintain a high average speed and ease of control, it was much sought after by the keen sportsman; its maximum speed was anything up to about 90 mph."

A masterpiece of visual excitement, the 500 K special sports roadster.
THE MUSEUM OF AUTOMOBILES

If customers chose to enjoy the sporting aspects of the "K" type over its normal touring value, Ferdinand Porsche, unlike Marc Birkigt, was not reluctant about satisfying them. In 1927, for those "keen sportsmen," he re-worked the "K" concept into a pure sports car. Not just another sports car, but perhaps the greatest sports car of his or any other age. First, Porsche dropped the new "S" type chassis as low as he could by arching the frame over the rear axle and using underslung rear springs. Then he turned his attention to a suitable engine, increasing displacement to 6.8 litres, fitting dual carburetors, and souping up the supercharger to get 180 hp and speed well over 100 mph. The car was very flexible (3 to 103 mph in top gear in standard tune) and, with the exception of the rather dubious brakes, was the very essence of classic sports motoring. The big, strong chassis could carry the heaviest formal coachwork and the powerful supercharged six-cylinder engine could push it faster than any limousine needed to travel. But, from the perspective of nearly half a century later, it seems a consummate waste to have put anything but the "typical," gaunt sports body of the mid-twenties on this magnificent chassis. Despite their obvious devotion to brute strength—plus a certain streak of arrogance—the "S" type Mercedes-Benz sports cars had enormous cachet and presence. Even people who know nothing about automobiles sense that they are in rarified air when they come upon one of the great white Mercedes sports cars of the golden age. They were big, hardy cars, but with their own kind of chic. Ettore Bugatti's crack about Monsieur Bentley building very fast trucks could not have been aimed at the equally robust Mercedes-Benz sports cars with anywhere near the same effect.

The "S" cars were not simply imposing playtoys for millionaires who enjoyed terrifying pedestrians by kicking on the blower in populated areas. Not only were they very effective sports cars but also one of the very few cars which could be run as full Grand Prix machines. The "S" started off by promptly winning the 1927 German Grand Prix at the brand new Nurburgring (1-2-3 in the large car class) and in the following year, according to Daimler-Benz, "scored 53 victories and set 17 records during the 1928 season, including the German sports record of 110.4 mph."

Ferdinand Porsche was a prodigious worker. He was at Daimler-Benz only five years, although his influence there makes it seem longer, and in that time he worked on sixty-five projects. For 1928 one of them was a successor to the "S," the even more *puissant* "SS," or Super Sport. The "SS" was simply more of a good thing—a logical progression of the Porsche philosophy of sports cars at that point in his career. Specifically, that meant a 7.1-litre engine being fed by a ten-pound supercharger, some 225 hp, and a quite unsettling meas-

A very attractive Type 290 cabriolet which has been three years in restoration by its present owner, Mr. M. L. Bud Cohn of Los Angeles.

ure of acceleration and speed. And if all this wasn't quite enough you could order—for $13,550 per chassis—the ultimate Porsche-designed sports car ever sold over the counter, the Super Sport Kurz or "SSK" with a foot and a half lopped out of the middle of the frame. The total effect of this machine—sharp vee-radiator, louvered hood, three big nickeled external exhausts, triple-laced wire wheels—was the feeling of being in the presence of a masterpiece of sculpture.

At the end of 1928 Ferdinand Porsche left Daimler-Benz to pursue the next phase of his multi-faceted career. He left in charge Hans Nibel, Benz's chief engineer who had joined the new company as part of the 1926 merger. Nibel had a long

One of the last of the 540 K sport cabriolets, built in 1939 and delivered to the Krupp family. Presently owned by James Leake of Muskogee, Oklahoma.

COURTESY M. L. BUD COHN

and distinguished career behind him at *Benz und Cie.* and his projects included the great Blitzen Benz record car of 1909 and his brilliantly advanced floating-axle racing car of 1923. Under him another great, but quite different, epoch in Mercedes-Benz history was to flower. Again it was a smooth transition to a new man at the helm, and at first Nibel seemed merely to pick up where Porsche left off. In fact, it was left to Nibel to bring Porsche's "S" cars to their final expression, the "SSKL." Nibel fitted the "SSK" with a high lift counterbalanced crankshaft, brought the *Kompressor* pressure up to twelve pounds (the famous "elephant blower"), and then punched holes in the frame to lighten the chassis. In doing so he created a 156-mph legend* which was all the more ethereal because, although the SSKL cars were raced prominently, they never seem to have been actually offered for public sale. At

* An aerodynamic SSKL was taken to that speed by Manfred von Brauchitsch at the Avus track in 1932.

Louver work on an "S" Type Mercedes-Benz; coachwork by Buhne of Berlin.

AUTHOR'S PHOTO

any rate, the SSKL was a very substantial sort of legend and in the years 1931–32 achieved twenty-eight wins for the three-pointed star, chief among them Rudolf Caracciola's signal victory in the 1931 *Mille Miglia.*

The SSKL was the last of the fire-breathing Mercedes-Benz sports cars. In the 1930s there occurred a polarization of competition cars at one end of the scale and touring and sports/touring cars at the other. When Mercedes-Benz decided to enter Grand Prix racing in 1934 under the new 750-kilogram formula, it began a whole series of esoteric Grand Prix cars which bore no resemblance to the new line of passenger and sports cars which Nibel had started. The GP cars, which brought enormous success to Mercedes racing efforts from 1934 to 1939, are quite beyond the scope of this book but Nibel's sports—or at least sporting—cars are among the most sought after machines of the golden age. Dr. Nibel's great specialty was springing and suspension and soon after he be-

The Porsche hand at work: 6.8 supercharged litres under the hood of the "S" Type Mercedes-Benz.

AUTHOR'S PHOTO

came chief engineer he began experimenting with a new independent suspension system. In 1931 the system was first offered on the 170, a small 1.7-litre, six-cylinder car introduced at just the right moment. Hard times were beginning to make their mark on companies producing only big, expensive, luxury cars, and in this depressed market Daimler-Benz came out with a mini luxury car with superior ride and roadholding, Mercedes prestige and a $2000 price tag. It was a success from the beginning and modified versions of the original car were built into the 1950s. Nibel's swing axle, independent suspension quickly proved itself on the 170 and was obviously destined for bigger and better things.

The first of these came in 1933 with the Type 380 sports coupe, a supercharged straight-eight 90/120 hp car with Nibel's swing axle at the rear and independently sprung front wheels with wishbones and coil springs. It was a quite different breed of animal from the "S" cars, less forceful and more refined, with the emphasis on comfortable and elegant transport rather than hill climbs and races. Along somewhat similar lines was a less expensive 2.9-litre, six-cylinder, side-valve car called the 290 which also shared a measure of the graceful curves of the 380.

Dr. Hans Nibel died in 1934, the year in which his concept of the superbly sprung grand touring car flowered into the 500 K, an enlarged 5-litre 100/160 hp development of the 380 in which the "K" now stood for *Kompressor* rather than *kurz*. Seven models of this great car were originally offered in 1934 ranging from a sports roadster to a four-door sedan. Hopefully, Dr. Nibel saw what Daimler-Benz's own coachbuilders at Sindelfingen had on the drawing boards for 1935, the 500 K "Special Roadster" which was quite likely the most beautiful and best balanced sports body ever put on a chassis anywhere —and it was a standard production catalogue model, not a one-of-a-kind custom creation! It would probably have satisfied the purists more if the big 7.1-litre "SSK" engine had been under the hood of the 500 K "Special Roadster" instead of the 5-litre, pushrod, overhead-valve straight-eight. Such crossbreeding would certainly have brightened its performance, but it is doubtful if anything could have added an ounce to the unique charisma of the magnificent body. In 1936 the 500 K escalated into the 540 K and what the Daimler-Benz catalogue described as "an international conception of beauty and speed." It was a less dramatic difference than there had been between the 380 and 500 K two years before, but the car served as the final expression of the Mercedes-Benz interpretation of what a gentleman's civilized sports car should be like in the last days of the golden age.

Chapter 12

ETTORE BUGATTI-AT THE ZENITH

If Ettore Bugatti had lived in the sixteenth century it is more than likely that he would have produced something on the order of the Mona Lisa and that his name would have been celebrated with Michelangelo, Botticelli and Cellini. On the other side of the coin, if Leonardo Da Vinci had lived in the twentieth century it is equally likely that he would have built Bugatti-like automobiles. Like Da Vinci, Bugatti was an artist by nature and an engineer by instinct; and by temperament he was an arch-individualist. It was a rare, probably unique, combination of talents in a creator of automobiles, even in an age more friendly to individualism than our own. The result was a small number of Bugatti automobiles—only about 6000 in all—which were totally unlike all other cars before or since.

Around these cars, and the memory of their creator, has grown a mystique. For the true *Bugattiste* Bugatti is still *le Patron* and his will unquestioned, and for his cars there is an aura of reverence and veneration seldom seen beyond monastic walls. Although Bugatti was notably successful in accumulating racing victories, the aura is certainly not built on that alone. Even at the zenith of its spectacular success the Bugatti was hardly an invincible machine. For all the glories there were matching failures and despairs, sometimes traceable to nothing else than Bugatti's refusal to profit from other men's minds (well, hardly ever) and to do things his way and his alone. Likewise, the appeal is not attributable to the practicality of his cars. The much told tale of an owner complaining to Bugatti that his car wouldn't start in cold weather and being advised from the court at Molsheim to invest in a heated garage is typical of both the man and his product. Comments about the stopping qualities of some models (Bugatti used cable brakes right up to World War II) brought assertions that Bugattis were intended to go, not to stop. Even as eminent an observer on the automotive scene as Colonel J. R. Buckley admits to being confounded by the religion of Bugattism. Probably the closest that any of the unbaptized will come to understanding is simply to say that a *Bugattiste* accepts the natural divinity of a Bugatti purely on faith, simply because it *is* a Bugatti.

As we have seen, Bugatti busied himself immediately after the war with racing, and manufacturing his 16-valve four-cylinder sports car. But he was anxious to get into an 8-cylinder car *de novo*, perhaps a bit too anxious. The first eight which Bugatti laid before the public late in 1921 was the enigmatic Type 28. This was a fascinating experiment which among various other innovations (such as an adjustable steering wheel and a two-speed transaxle) included Bugatti's first and only departure from cable brakes, to front hydraulics. But, noble try though it was, the car remained just that—an expensive experiment—and was never produced for sale. For the following year's round of shows, however, the real thing was ready. This was the Type 30—a smaller, less expensive two-litre car which, while certainly not one of the great Bugattis, was still an important one. It was Bugatti's first production straight-eight and the first car in which he began to pay close attention to the sculptural purity of his engine compartment.

In its debut the Type 30 received mixed reviews. Charles

Faroux, one of the most influential names in French motoring, went into flights of Gallic ecstasy over it . . . "I cannot imagine anything which could give me more joy than this experience with my two-litre Bugatti!" Others were not so enthusiastic, pointing to the high noise and vibration levels and to the reluctance of the Type 30 to halt when commanded. The pedal worked on the front-wheel brakes and the handbrake on the rear wheels, so the driver was left to work out his own compromises about deceleration. Yet, the car was so typically Bugatti—responsive, agile, and willing—that people tended to forgive it much of its shortcomings once they got to know it. It was sufficient that the Type 30

The Type 30, introduced in 1922, was Bugatti's first production straight-eight. It had casual brakes, and only three crankshaft bearings and a high level of noise and vibration, but drivers were willing to forgive it a lot because of its fine roadholding.

MONTAGU MOTOR MUSEUM

The Type 37 A, a 15-litre, four-cylinder, supercharged GP car which was a variant of the eight-cylinder Type 35 and served as a successor to the earlier Brescia of similar displacement. The Type 37/37 A was one of those Bugattis which could alternate as a full racing or sports car as the owner chose.

BRIGGS CUNNINGHAM AUTOMOTIVE MUSEUM

gave its owners moments of private pleasure, rather than impressing strangers. A satisfied Englishman, talking about low-speed torque in his car, summed it up nicely: "Anyone who buys a Bugatti of any model to crawl up and down Bond Street and edify its frequenters . . . is not really a discerning person."

The Type 30 had some combat experience on fields of battle from nearby Strasbourg to faraway Indianapolis, but did not greatly distinguish itself either at home or abroad. The Indianapolis cars which ran in 1923 impressed the spectators with their characteristic fine cornering ability but there was an epidemic of snapping connecting rods among the five Bu-

In the Type 35 Bugatti struck off a completely balanced and integrated machine of masterwork calibre. Besides being an enormously successful competition car on both GP and sports circuits, the Type 35 qualified as a legitimate *objet d'art.*

BRIGGS CUNNINGHAM AUTOMOTIVE MUSEUM

gattis and only one survived the "500" to finish ninth. On home ground in the 1922 French Grand Prix, held nearly in Bugatti's backyard that year, the result was better: second and third place. For this race, *le Patron* had devised some rather un-Bugatti-like but interesting racing bodies that looked like aerial bombs with wheels. They had blunt torpedo noses with a circular air hole for the radiator—which made them look like jet engines head on—and long graceful wasp tails with the exhaust coming out the tip. Contemporary reports indicated that the Bugattis smoked a lot, so they must have given the futuristic appearance of some kind of flying rocket bomb. Bugatti's cars at the next year's French Grand Prix at Tours were again esoteric: aerodynamic, so-called "tank cars" which swept up from the road surface in an elongated curve to only 31 inches above the road and back down to the road again in a similar curve at the rear. In profile, they were like a cross section cut out of an airplane wing, with perfectly straight sides. While they were not especially pretty, they were menacing, almost cruel looking machines and that was certainly the impression they left on their drivers who remembered them as motorized torture chambers. Against stiff competition, the "tank" Bugattis returned a third place in the

LES GARNITURES
FERODO
LES PROJECTEURS CODE
CIBIE
Spido
N 30
BOWES

1923 French Grand Prix. The idea behind these cars was basically sound, although ahead of its time, and Bugatti revived the principle again, more successfully, a dozen years later. But for the moment he had other ideas in mind.

Those ideas were certainly among the best that Bugatti ever had, resulting in what many *cognescenti* regard as *the* Bugatti —the immortal Type 35 and its variants. A weak spot of the Type 30 was its too-few crankshaft bearings (there were only three!). In the Type 35, Bugatti rectified this with an adequate sprinkling of roller bearings throughout, retaining the same straight-eight, two-litre measurements. With these changes and his own style of delivering lubricant under pressure to the bearings, he answered the complaints leveled against the Type 30. But the new engine was only a part of the new car.

What Bugatti was doing here was not merely revising the relatively mediocre Type 30 but striking off a completely balanced and integrated machine of masterwork calibre. The chassis itself was a piece of jewelry, and curious in that the crankcase was merged into a pair of cross-members so that in addition to supporting the engine the crankcase itself also served to strengthen the frame. Also, the crankcase was pierced by a series of thirteen tubes through which air flowed to help cool the oil. But of this finely wrought jewelry the crown jewel had to be the front axle. This was a piece of philosophy archtypical of Bugatti, and a piece of work guaranteed to strike cold fear into the heart of an engineer who had to work within a normal sort of manufacturing establishment without the total freedom of Molsheim. To create his famous axle, which remained basically standard on all subsequent cars, Bugatti began with a bar of high grade steel and drilled it

A flurry of Bugattis at the Monaco Grand Prix in 1930. In this period the single-overhead-cam Grand Prix cars were facing stiffening competition, and Bugatti's reply was the double-overhead-cam Type 51, which still retained the simplistic beauty of the earlier Type 35.

DAIMLER-BENZ A.G.

A choice collection of Molsheim machinery. Left: Type 37, 1.5-litre, four-cylinder Grand Prix racer. Middle: Type 51, Bugatti's great double-overhead-cam Grand Prix car, 2.3-litre, straight-eight. Right: Type 59, 3.3-litre straight-eight Grand Prix racer derived from the Type 57.

MONTAGU MOTOR MUSEUM

through. Then the ends were forged solid, redrilled to a smaller diameter, and slotted with square openings for the front springs to pass *through* the axle. Then the axle was bent and forged into final shape. It was practical, functional, beautiful—and pure Bugatti.

And then there was the matter of wheels for the Type 35. Fans of today's "mag" wheels may do a double take at the Type 35's wheels, and repeat it when they look even closer. The wheels are visually very striking, with eight wide aluminum "spokes" with just enough pitch to feed air into the brake drums. Looking closer one finds that the wheel and brake drum were cast as a single unit. The dual value of Bugatti's unique wheel was that it helped to dissipate heat better than conventional methods, and that when a race car pulled into the pits for a tire change it could also get new brake shoes in a few seconds more.

Bugatti Type 55 sports roadster; 2.3-litre straight-eight, supercharged.

BRIGGS CUNNINGHAM AUTOMOTIVE MUSEUM

An extraordinary car should project an extraordinary image and it was here, in the realm of balance and proportion and aesthetics, that *le Patron* was without peer. Bugatti succeeded as few designers ever have in distilling the pure essence of functional beauty and transferring it from drafting paper to metal. The Type 35 was a beautiful creation, beautiful not simply as a car but as a legitimate *objet d'art.* After the talents of Bugatti, the engineer, had been spent on the engine, chassis, and wheels, the talents of Bugatti, the artist, took over. The result was sculpture, a piece of art that could move at 114 mph.

When Bugatti prepared his Type 35s for their maiden race he kept in mind that he was readying an art object as well as a car, and he groomed his team of five cars as few racing machines have ever been groomed to take a starter's flag. *Le*

Under the hood of *La Royale;* 12.7 litres and five feet of engine turned aluminum sculpture.

AUTHOR'S PHOTO

Bugatti's excursion into the Grand Baroque, the Type 41 Royale. Although an enormous luxury car, the Royale leaned on the lessons which Bugatti learned on the race courses, and was a remarkably light and efficient car for its size.

MR. J. LEMON BURTON, ESQ.

Marque Bugatti faced the dirt and danger of the Lyons course of the 1924 French Grand Prix with pride—and polished steel axles, burnished nickel radiators, buffed aluminum wheels, and waxed French racing-blue lacquer on the elegant bodywork. Bugatti himself described the cars as being of "irreproachable finish, fine appearance, and perfectly developed." Bugatti laid out a plan to capture victory in the Grand Prix which, in his own description, sounded like a campaign out of Caesar's *Gallic Wars.* Moving overland in a caravan from Molsheim to Lyons—which included running the Type 35s under their own power—Bugatti brought in some 30 tons of assorted impedimenta. There was a self contained support system for 45 people including refrigerators, showers, a portable kitchen, and food for a month. The racing world had never seen anything quite like it, and wouldn't again until Alfred Neubauer took over the Mercedes-Benz racing team in the thirties.

Not far into the race Robert Burns' warning about best

laid plans began to come true. Pierre de Vizcaya did not even complete the first round of the circuit before he had a flat and rolled into the pits on a rim. It was another strength of the Bugatti cast wheel that it could be driven on without air pressure in the tire and without damaging the wheel, within reason. Under race conditions it did exactly this for de Vizcaya. But then on his third lap it was called upon to repeat the performance when the entire tread of a tire left the rim and wrapped around de Vizcaya's steering wheel, nearly causing an accident. For this race Bugatti had chosen a new pattern Dunlop tire which seemed best suited to his special wheels. Ironically, the batch used in the race itself suffered from bad vulcanization and were literally disintegrating before Bugatti's eyes. As he watched stoically, a tread flipped off Costantini's car and smashed into the gear shift lever so hard that the driver could use only first and third gears and shortly had to withdraw. When another tire similarly failed on de Vizcaya's car, it skidded and smashed into a house at

Type 57 engine, double-overhead-camshaft, 3.3 litres.

AUTHOR'S PHOTO

the roadside. de Vizcaya was unhurt but, in Bugatti's words, was "heartbroken" at the sight of the mangled little Type 35.

Despite constant tire changing—for which Bugatti profusely praised his pit crew—*le Patron* lost three of his five cars to tire trouble and so much time that the remaining two finished only seventh and eighth. It was a moment of deep discouragement for Bugatti. He wrote a long apologetic letter to his dealers and customers in which he recounted the experience at Lyons, explained the merits of his car and its wheels (which the ignorant had blamed for the tire trouble), and promised better things for the future. Despite the anguish which the defective tires had caused him he did not speak vindictively about them, nor even mention the maker's name.

When Bugatti promised his friends and customers that his car would redeem itself, it is unlikely that even he envisioned what would really happen. Over the next few years the Type 35 revealed itself not only as possibly the most beautiful car in history but also as a likely candidate for the winningest. One of the Type 35's first celebrated victories after Lyons was the next year's Targa Florio, the tortuous and demanding race through the Sicilian mountains. To win the Targa Florio once was a grand accomplishment, but Bugatti took it for five consecutive years. And it was just the beginning. In 1926 *le Marque Bugatti* recorded an even dozen Grand Prix victories, and for 1927 alone Bugatti claimed some two thousand sporting successes of various kinds.

Although teams from Molsheim accounted for their share of these incredible statistics, it is obvious that no manufacturer, not even with resources many times Bugatti's, could pursue racing on this scale. Much of the stuffing of the record books with the name Bugatti was due to private owners who bought and raced their cars with their own money, sometimes with factory assistance which was also bought and paid for. Naturally, private or professional drivers had a choice of any maker who produced high performance cars, but many soon found that Monsieur Bugatti treated his customers quite differently from any other maker, either before or since.

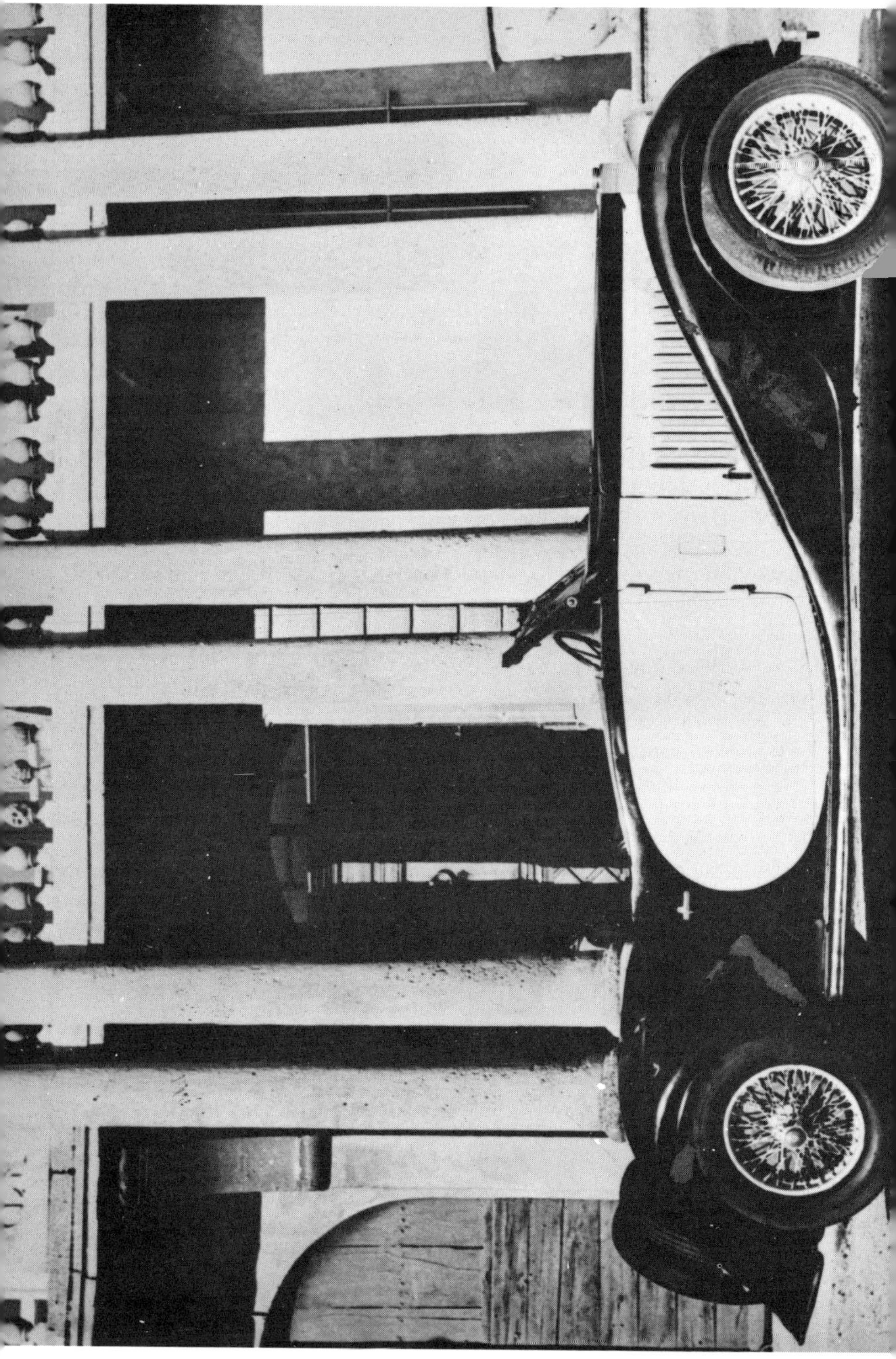

Basically, Bugatti's policy was that he believed in doing as much for his customers as he did for himself. He was a bit selective about just *who* could buy a Bugatti, and once supposedly refused to sell a car to the king of Albania because he didn't like his manners and felt that a Bugatti in his possession would tarnish the Molsheim reputation. The general policy of most makers about racing machines, particularly Grand Prix racers, at the time was that a company would spend a great deal of money to develop and build a few highly specialized cars to formula specifications (with little reference to production models) and field these cars with factory hired drivers in an attempt to cover the marque's public image with glory—and sales appeal. Usually, the only time a private buyer could get his hands on such cars was when the maker had built something better. At Molsheim things were done differently. Provided that you had sufficient cash and social acceptance, you could come to Molsheim, stay at Bugatti's private hotel for customers (run by his daughter), eat food prepared by his personally selected chef, drink wines and plum brandy from Bugatti's own vineyards and distillery, visit the museum housing his brother Rembrandt Bugatti's sculpture, and eventually drive out in a full Grand Prix car identical to the ones which *le Patron* himself sent into battle. It was, from all points of view, a unique opportunity. There are no parallels to it today.

Bugatti invited the seriously curious to Molsheim "to see for yourself what you would not find in any other car factory in the world—that my racing cars are production models, and that even my tourers have the same engines and mechanism as my racing cars, are built of the same materials, and are assembled by the same workmen." Speaking specifically about the Type 35, Bugatti claimed that "it has been built on the same principle as all the others, since I do not propose

A Type 57 with "torpedo" coachwork. The Type 57 was a joint project of Ettore and Jean Bugatti, combining the elder Bugatti's expertise gathered over his entire career and the younger Bugatti's skill as designer and administrator.

Type 57 sports coupe. The Type 57 was the last production car and represented Bugatti's concept of a practical and efficient car which appealed to wider numbers of people. About 750 of several varieties were built, a large number by Molsheim measure.

COURTESY MR. ERIC SORENSEN

ever to race with a machine that is not strictly that which the customer can buy."

The Type 35 was not really one car but several, for it went through a series of developments and variations with different displacements, gear and compression ratios, and, in some models, superchargers, in spite of Bugatti's famous reluctance about blown engines. In all there were nine such versions of the basic Type 35.

Bugatti did not see the Type 35 exclusively as a Grand Prix car; in fact, he wrote about it at the time of Lyons that "This car must not be considered as a racing car. . . . One can use them in town as easily as in any race." This was another of the unique aspects of Bugatti's cars. It was sometimes difficult to define where Grand Prix cars left off and

The *pièce de resistance* of Ettore Bugatti's sports cars and the finale of Jean Bugatti's career as a body designer; the magnificent *Atlantique* electron coupe. This car was sold recently.

PHOTO BY STROTHER MAC MINN,
COURTESY SOTHEBY, PARKE-BERNET, LOS ANGELES

sports cars began. There were cases where a car which had just run in a Grand Prix event was fitted with fenders and windscreen and then run in a sports car race. Drawing a line between sports and touring Bugattis could also be mystifying at times.

But whether Ettore Bugatti chose to extol its virtues as a town car or not, the Type 35 was perhaps a bit much car (and money) for some drivers who thought in terms of something more like the old Brescia. For them Bugatti created the Type 40, a four-cylinder 1.5-litre which, though a much tamer car, profited from experience with the Type 35 and sold for the very modest chassis price of about $1600. For the money one got up to 75 mph, much better brakes than the

Brescia or Type 30 (at last), good fuel economy, a somewhat stand-offish gearbox, impeccable Bugatti road manners, and a selection of some very pretty little roadster and coupe bodies. Considering the value received, most all Bugattis were good buys and the Type 40 especially so, even though the overly critical did tend to make fun of its comparative docility.

There is a complex continuity to Bugatti cars. One cannot help sensing the sympatico between two Bugattis which may be as much as a generation apart in origin. One model sometimes "matured" into another, and there was a good bit of crossbreeding between models, probably more than in any other marque. But it was not just genetic roulette; Bugatti had a genius for isolating the compatible concepts of different models and re-assembling them into a new car. Thus was born one of the best loved Bugattis of all, the Type 43 Grand Sport which first appeared in 1927. The engine of this car was pretty much the Type 35 B, a supercharged 2.3-litre, straight-eight used to win the 1926 Targa Florio, and the chassis was closely patterned on the Type 38, a touring model introduced in 1926 to replace the old Type 30. A touring chassis under a Grand Prix class engine was for most designers a suspicious combination but coming from Bugatti the result was one of the great sports cars of all time.

The English motor writer W. F. Bradley, who spent many happy hours both at Molsheim and behind the wheel of its product, called his personal Type 43 "A racing car with a touring body," and went into paeans over the car. He describes a maximum speed of 112 mph and idyllic long stretches at over ninety on the empty *Routes National* in the late twenties, adding that "the greatest pleasure is obtained not in attempting to obtain the maximum from it, but in its wonderful acceleration, its high degree of flexibility, and its remarkable steadiness at speed, and particularly when one is negotiating hills." Later, he recounts an interesting test of the Type 43's flexibility: he put the car in top gear, turned on the ignition and moved away "by using the electric starter, and gaining speed rapidly." In this way the car would reach 82 mph in

54 seconds, *without* using the gearbox. With conventional shifting, 80 mph could be reached in 25 seconds. Bradley also claimed that his own Type 43 had been driven "right across France without use of the gears." These qualities plus service accessibility and a lack of temperament (at least for a Bugatti) add up to one of the most sought after of all Bugattis.

In 1927, near the height of his glory, Bugatti launched a project which carried him straight into the age of the grand baroque. This was La Royale, the ultimate car from Molsheim —or from anywhere else. As the final expression of a luxury carriage (originally for sale only to royalty and heads of state), the Type 41 Royale was not properly a sports car. Yet the car inherited so much from Bugatti's ventures on the track that it was also a world apart from an ordinary heavy, dour limousine. With 12.7 litres of straight-eight, overhead-cam engine to put things in motion, weight saving and competition car efficiency hardly seemed a necessity, yet Bugatti used the same efficient philosophy that guided the high-strung Type 35 race cars. The five-foot-long engine—neat, angular aluminum—weighed only 770 pounds; the cast iron block, 238 pounds, and the crankshaft, 220 pounds. The whole chassis, on a 170-inch wheelbase, weighed only 3850 pounds, amazingly only a thousand pounds more than a 4.5-litre Bentley sports! The torque was prodigious, giving some 300 hp at only 1700 rpm, and the speed was limited only by the judgment of the driver, especially since Bugatti considered a speedometer superfluous. An enquiry from an Arab prince brought the reply that "The car can attain any speed desired by the designer." Actually, about 125 mph was on tap if asked, and with some aerodynamic body design 140 was theoretically possible. Only six Royales were built (with several re-bodyings) and of these two qualify at least as semi-sports cars: a roadster for a French manufacturer (Bugatti finally had relented about selling only to crowned heads) and a sports cabriolet for a German doctor. One can only dream about an all-out sports Royale with special compression and gear ratios and supercharger!

The high efficiency double-overhead-cam engine as Ernest Henry had devised it for the Grand Prix Peugeot two years before World War I had become *de rigeur* for high performance cars after the war. In fact, England's Sunbeam had a production double-overhead-cam sports car on the market by 1925. Yet Ettore Bugatti stubbornly ignored the double-overhead-cam all through the 1920s. When he finally gave in, he studied an American Miller racing design (which he considered the best of the lot) and then—typically Bugatti—proceeded to install his first twin-cam engine in a touring car! Some touring car! Sharing the chassis of the Type 46, a down-scaled version of *La Royale*, the Type 50 was powered with a 4.9-litre, supercharged, double-overhead-cam engine rated in excess of 200 hp and offered breath-taking acceleration. Fortunately for all concerned a much more logical short-wheelbase Type 50 Grand Sport version was also made.

With his double-overhead-cam engine Bugatti began another epoch as he had with the single-overhead-cam Type 35, and the inevitable crossbreeding and revising of double-overhead-cam engines and various chassis began. It eventually included a not very successful attempt at a four-wheel-drive car and a new racing car of questionable balance and stability (the Type 54), both of which are best let alone. Much more fruitful routes led to the Type 51, Bugatti's first twin-cam competition car, and a gilding of the lily that was the great Type 35. The Type 51, issued in 2-litre, 2.3-litre, and 1.5-litre editions, incorporated some engine refinements into the new double-overhead-cam design and retained the eye-filling cast aluminum wheels, also strengthened and improved. Visually the car was identical to the elegant Type 35.

For 1932 Bugatti was at it again, dropping the Type 51

Jean Bugatti's *Coupe Atlantique* built of "electron" alloy almost seemed out of the Buck Rogers comics of its day, yet was done with consummate skill and taste. Out of the 750 or so Type 57s built, only four were *Atlantiques*.

PHOTO BY STROTHER MAC MINN,
COURTESY SOTHEBY, PARKE-BERNET, LOS ANGELES

This *Atlantique* had modifications to the rear windows by Carrozzeria Motto in Turin in 1954 which improved visibility.
PHOTO BY STROTHER MAC MINN,
COURTESY SOTHEBY, PARKE-BERNET, LOS ANGELES

Grand Prix engine into the Type 54 Grand Prix chassis to create another car, the Type 55. But this time there were two Bugattis on the project, Bugatti senior and his son Jean. Bugatti the younger introduced a new element onto the Molsheim scene. Inheriting fully his father's flair for line and style, he tempered it with technology, and perhaps he eventually came to have a little firmer grasp on the world as it really was than his more romantic father had. As he became more and more active in the "affairs of state" at Molsheim, Jean brought great joy to Ettore Bugatti: heights of joy to be matched by depths of sorrow.

Even beyond his father's contribution to the Type 35—which was 0 to 50 mph in 8.7 seconds with exhilarating pick-up all the way up to 115 mph—Jean's contribution as body designer was sufficient *raison d'être* for the car. The Type 55 was catalogued as the "Super Sport," although anyone who had to be told that it was a sports car had probably stopped breathing. By 1932 styling trends were toward flowing, svelte lines and in Jean Bugatti's interpretation of what an open two-seater should look like every line seems to fall perfectly into place. It was another of those rare cars of elemental beauty that will always remain vital. Yet even beyond that, the Type 55 Super Sport seems the very soul of what a sports car should look like.

The Type 55's performance—high speed quickly reached and easily held—was as much appreciated by drivers as was its grace by connoisseurs. But even this was just a teaser, a curtain raiser for what was about to come from Molsheim: Ettore Bugatti's *grand travail*, the Type 57 and its descendants.

Much like W.O. Bentley's cars, the Type 57 did not begin life as a high strung sports car but as a high grade touring car which drew upon competition experience. The first thoughts about the Type 57 were toward a highly refined and civilized personal car, and so the old high decibel ball and roller bearings were left behind so that the new 3.3-litre, double-overhead-cam engine (later rubber mounted) emitted more "cultured" noises. With suggestions from Jean Bugatti, the car evolved in the direction of a more practical machine with appeal to people beyond the inner circle of aficionados, yet at the same time preserved the unique Bugatti virtues. Technically, some of these virtues had perhaps been preserved beyond their time, yet they worked for *le Patron* as they worked for no other man. While much less grand cars than Bugattis now had hydraulic brakes, the Type 57 made its debut still with the usual cable-operated stopping system; yet nobody complained about Bugatti braking. Eventually, however, the conversion to hydraulics came—a few months before the end of production. Also, while other people were going over to independent front suspension (even staid old Rolls-Royce) Bugatti stuck to his tubular front axle—polished and plated, *mais certainment*—although after some experiments he provided a split axle modification to give a token of independent front suspension. But again, even with sculpture instead of technology between the front wheels, no reasonable man could find fault with the road manners of the Type 57. So even when he decided to "go modern" with a practical car (by Bugatti standards!) by producing basically the one model and its variants, Ettore Bugatti was still Ettore Bugatti.

The earliest Type 57s arrived in the spring of 1934 and fulfilled the Bugatti expectations. The acceleration on the road—right up to the top speed of 90 plus—was nearly matched by the acceleration of the upward sales curve. It was a good omen, especially for sluggish times, and ultimately Jean Bugatti's concepts were vindicated in those sales charts as production reached 750, very impressive by Molsheim measure. As a Grand Touring car the Type 57 was eminently successful, but the following year the inevitable sports version, the Type 57 S, appeared. Technically, it was not a far step from the Type 57 to the sports version, merely a matter of revising compression ratios from 6.3:1 up to 8.3(8.7):1 and rear axle ratios from 4.17:1 to 3.85:1. But visually the two cars were a world apart, owing to a lower and shorter chassis under the Type 57 S and a revised oval-outline vee-shaped radiator. That may well have offended the faithful (although there had been other deviations in the radiator design before) but the overall effect of the new frontal aspect with the Jean Bugatti-designed sports bodies was electrifying. The low-slung headlights faired into the bodywork beside the fenders added to the low, lithe look and gave the car a stylishly sinister flavor. Here was the ideal conveyance for playboys all over the western world, or James Bondian spies, pre-World War II vintage. Actually, there were at least two Bond types who did drive Bugattis—Robert Benoist, and an Englishman named Grover-Williams who reputedly operated a wartime espionage organization from an address in Avenue Montaigne which was coincidentally the Paris residence of Ettore Bugatti. When Benoist was once being taken in for questioning by the Gestapo, as the story goes, he talked the German officer into letting him drive his own car back to headquarters. For his naiveté the officer got an excellent demonstration of the acceleration of a supercharged Bugatti, and lost his prisoner.

In perfectly standard form the Type 57 offered as much power and road finesse as most drivers would ever need. Yet, for the modest few who could handle it, a supercharger was added for 1936 and the model was catalogued as the Type 57 C. The obvious extension was of course the inevitable Type 57 SC, the supercharged sports version which appeared the following year. Competition models of the Type 57 generally cleaned up at the races, and Bugatti's grand triumph at the 1939 Le Mans was a sort of reply in kind to the Mercedes-Benz/Auto-Union monopoly of the Grand Prix circuits once ruled by the sky blue cars. For Le Mans a standard Type 57 C chassis was fitted with an aerodynamic body, an oil cooler, and a revised rear axle ratio quoted to give over 142 mph. The car ran like a watch throughout the twenty-four hours to finish first at an average of 86.8 mph.

It was a great day for Bugatti, and the last such that he would ever see. Within a few weeks dual disaster waited to wring the very heart and soul of *le Patron* of Molsheim. The soul went out of Bugatti's world in August 1939 when Jean was killed driving the Le Mans car on a test run for another race; and the heart of it stopped beating not long afterward when the war ended the last era that would permit an artist to build automobiles.

The Golden Age had passed.

About the Author

Louis William Steinwedel is well known to aficionados of classic, antique and sports cars who read the national motor magazines. His articles there, always written from first-hand knowledge of his car-subjects, and with unusual charm (which adds something to automotive writing), appeal to readers who appreciate having more than nuts-and-bolts to contend with . . . the Steinwedel touch.

The author professes to work at the Law, but those who know him will argue the point that his heart belongs to the more romantic things of life—more to torque than to tort. Among his interests are handcrafted antique guns which he collects, and, of course, the great cars which he admires and drives when he can, and about which he will write at the drop of a law book.

The Golden Age of Sports Cars is Mr. Steinwedel's third book, and follows *The Mercedes-Benz Story* and *The Duesenberg*, the latter written in collaboration with J. Herbert Newport, former Duesenberg designer.